Thirteen
Bad Years

*To Robin —
a cure for insomnia*

Larry

Thirteen Bad Years

A Curious Layman's
Look at the United States
Between 1763 and 1776

L.J. Nee

Copyright © 2004 by L.J. Nee.

ISBN: Softcover   1-4134-6038-0

All rights reserved. No part of this book may be reproduced or transmitted in any form or by any means, electronic or mechanical, including photocopying, recording, or by any information storage and retrieval system, without permission in writing from the copyright owner.

This book was printed in the United States of America.

To order additional copies of this book, contact:
Xlibris Corporation
1-888-795-4274
www.Xlibris.com
Orders@Xlibris.com

DEDICATED to my wife and children who have heard about "the book" for years. Such as it is, here it is at long last.

"What do we mean by the Revolution? The war with Britain? That was no part of the Revolution: it was only the effect and consequence of it. The revolution was in the minds and hearts of the people—before a drop of blood was shed at Lexington."
—John Adams

(Or maybe not)

Prologue

England.

It is only fitting and proper that any history of that part of the world that became the United States of America should begin with the word "England."

The thirteen colonies were, after all, not American colonies—they were English colonies in North America, founded and primarily populated by English, operating under English law and fashioning a variation of the English social structure.

Events now identified as pre-Revolutionary American history were principally reflections of the English domestic and foreign policies. Few purely domestic happenings generated actions (or reactions) any further away than adjoining colonies.

The thirteen colonies strung out along the western shore of the Atlantic Ocean were not even the only English colonies. There were nine others to the south as well as Ireland. With the close of the Seven Years War, there were also Canada and India.

To appreciate the flow or action over the period between the Peace of Paris (1763) and the Declaration of Independence (1776), action that changed the composition of the world, requires a backward look to set the stage.

Introduction

Reaching into the dim recesses of academic memory for the causes of the American Revolution, the author's residual impression was twofold: The English were incredibly stupid, naïve or uninformed in formulating foreign policy, especially as regarded their American colonies; on this side of the Atlantic, malcontents like Sam Adams were grinding out their pamphlets haranguing and agitating the colonists to insurrection and revolt.

Preliminary reintroduction to the period reminded me that it wasn't quite that simple, but did little to upset the basic recollection: English colonial policy (and the Provincials' reaction to it) was the largest single contributor to the war.

Prolonged exposure, however, began to introduce factors that sometimes explained or sometimes obscured the reasons for Britain's colonial policies, factors that had their roots in economics, religion and politics.

While the American Revolution was not a religious war per se, religion played a part in the founding of the majority of the original colonies, a larger role in some than others but always a factor that affected colonial thinking and behavior.

On the political and commercial side, advance warnings of probable, even certain, colonial resistance to various Parliamentary actions were given, but Parliament acted anyway. Cabinet officers judged overly sympathetic to colonial views seldom stayed long. English policy makers appeared at times obsessed with the possibility of American independence.

More extensive reading made it increasingly difficult to reconcile a globe-encircling mercantilist empire, with its emphasis on detailed bookkeeping and balance sheets, with a stupid, naïve or even misinformed administration. Once started, this train of thought led to the consideration of (and search for) other reasons behind Britain's colonial policy in the 1760s and 1770s.

Could the measures, although unpopular with the colonists, have been taken deliberately? Could some motive have driven England to risk the almost certain displeasure of the colonies? If so, what were they? As a corollary, the question occurred as to why the English were so apprehensive about an independence movement in America at a time when there were no apparent widespread demonstrations of it here? Or were there?

Then came the most surprising thought, at least to the author: Could the wave of independence that eventually swept the Thirteen Colonies have been inspired by the British preoccupation that it might happen, a kind of self-fulfilling prophecy? Would the hypothesis of British apprehension over American independence and their actions to prevent it provide an overall canopy under which British policies and acts might become understandable, even predictable?

Viewed in this light, England's attempts to control trade and commerce, currency, form of government and even migration to the colonies can be said to show a unified purpose. Against the theory of apprehension, it is argued that these steps were those usually followed in the erection of an empire under the mercantilist approach. Why then were they not taken consistently throughout the empire? Ireland was not taxed for revenue until she was represented in the House of Commons and the House of Lords. India was not governed by a royal governor and an elected assembly.

Could there be other possible explanations? Indeed, yes. Some lay the Revolution at the door of economics, the provincials' thirst for pounds and pence. Obviously, the theory goes, they could not be content with stringent enforcement of trade regulations. But an equally valid argument can be made against the English and their mercantilist economics, especially coupled with an inflated national debt and increased administrative costs after the Seven Years War.

Or possibly it was all a question of semantics. Maybe 3,000 miles between the colonists and the folks back home was having an adverse effect on their common language, to the point that they were using the same words on opposite sides of the Atlantic but with different meanings. Yet India, in those pre-Suez Canal days as far removed in time if not actual distance, did not seem to have the problem. Nor was there a language gap between north and south in the thirteen colonies.

It has been suggested that those endorsing independence over here were the conservative rather than the radicals as usually depicted; that they reached a stage of arrested development when they reduced their constitution (setting forth the limits of power for their colonial governments) to writing and holding those written constitutions relatively unchangeable. Their contemporaries in England, it is argued, followed the more liberal course by changing and modifying that body of common law and custom known as the English constitution. But resorting to arms to throw off the established government is not usually considered a conservative course of action.

Then, perhaps, the estrangement of the colonists was the unplanned byproduct of the political infighting between the powerful Whig families entrenched in Parliament and the supporters of the young, activist king. Yet the policies that contributed so much to this estrangement improved little following the installation of Lord North as the head of Parliament, the point in time at which George III is conceded to have effective control over Parliament's actions.

And then there is Toynbee's theory of challenge and response. But who was doing the challenging and who was responding?

Unfortunately, the author feels that as attractive as any of these theories might be in any particular instance, none alone will serve to explain the events between 1763 and 1776. At different times, and under different circumstances, it is possible to see first one motive force and then another rising to the surface. Yes, the English were apprehensive about American independence and it did affect some aspects of their colonial policy. In some parts of the colonies Americans were interested, even devoted, to making money. Parliament was worried about where the money was coming from to pay the national debt and maintain the empire. Americans, on the other hand, were worried about where the specie was coming from to maintain their commerce.

In short, there is no single, simple explanation for the events leading to the Revolution. This is not to indicate that it was an accident, a chance coming together of circumstances. This would stretch the law of coincidence beyond bursting, since it must be remembered that within 50 years all North American colonies with the exception of Canada and the Guianas shook off their home governments and gained their independence in the same manner as the United States.

It is in the hope of showing which combinations of motives produced which link in the chain of events that this is written.

If this is the direction of what follows, why start with the year 1763? Because it may be said with some justification that the history of the United States began in that year. What preceded was prologue. In advancing this contention, one must concede what insurance men refer to as "pre-existing conditions." Obviously, its physical history began centuries before. The North and South American continents had been discovered, claimed, explored and exploited. England, France, Spain, Holland and Sweden all had planted their colonies, warred over them, protected them, ignored them.

But as far as the United States is concerned, the political relations, the religious connections and the trade policies of 1763 were little different in a broad sense than they had been since 1607. Geographically, little had changed since 1732. For England, the year found her at the height of what has been called the First British Empire. She controlled North America, India and the high seas while her European rivals were reduced to near impotence.

Thirteen years later, however, a new nation had joined the world community and the English empire was reduced more greatly than anyone appreciated at the time.

The United States was not the result of ignorance on the one hand nor rabble rousing on the other. England was the mother, France the midwife and the years 1763 to 1776 its gestation period. We hope to find here who was the father.

Perhaps one of the reasons for ambiguity about the root causes of Great Britain's actions during the period preceding the American Revolution is the debate that has grown over the years about the motivations that drove George III.

The early histories are primarily by authors identified with the "Whig" label. These, naturally, attributed the worst of motives to the king since he came to the throne with the avowed intent of breaking the "Whig oligarchy" that had been in place many years.

Arguments rage about whether Whigs and Tories were, in fact, political parties during the period or whether the court-country was a more appropriate division. Since the early 1900s, the pendulum has swung back and forth as each theory advanced has had its detractors.

Much of this controversy has ranged among British historians. American historians, of course, have their own views, which are more homogenous than the British.

Digging for the motivation of men dead more than 200 years leaves the historian at the mercy of whatever written records survive. But even these are suspect. Official documents are official documents and are usually accepted at face value. But they generally give small evidence of the inner machinations that led to the document. Private letters and diaries, on the other hand, have to be viewed with a cautious eye. They are assuredly subject to the author's biases, knowledge or lack thereof, and interpretation of what knowledge he possesses. They could also be inspired by self-aggrandizement or even a desire to mislead or deceive.

So what is a person with a more than passing interest in the period to do?

My approach has been to read as widely as possible among the various schools of thought and try to extract from the thinking of dozens of professional historians those things that best fit what seems to be most logical and backed by historical fact.

Certain things happened. Why they happened is an interesting pursuit.

But one of the problems with reading history is that history is not neat. The reader finds himself drawn backward in time to find the roots of an event, the beginning of the string, as it were.

Therefore, to understand the three major threads that combine to weave the picture that was colonial America, we have to delve into Martin Luther's differences with the Catholic church, Henry VIII's marital problems and mercantilism in the 1600s as well as the politics of early 1700s and how each of these played out on both sides of the Atlantic.

Digressions they may be, but they are necessary digressions. At least, they were to me.

So let us embark, looking at the three threads in order of their beginnings as we set the stage for the 13 years of primary interest.

Chapter 1

It has been said that the business of business is business. It could be said with equal certainty that the business of empire is business. The possibility of wealth was as important to Europe's exploration of the globe as the natural inquisitiveness of man. Someone had to finance these early voyages of exploration and the incentive was normally monetary.

In face of that fact, if there is a label most commonly attached to the British Empire as it stood in 1763, it is "mercantilist," which is defined as a capitalistic system in which the mechanisms of trade were heavily controlled by the state rather than by market forces in order to accumulate national wealth. The underlying thought was that a country should sell as much as possible and buy as little as possible, thereby collecting the difference in hard currency and becoming rich.

As a corollary, it suited the exporting country to keep its labor costs as low as possible, making its exports cheaper. And, if the workers were making scant wages, it also kept the demand for imported goods low because the general public could not afford them.

A few well-chosen tariffs also helped restrict the flow of foreign goods and, if that didn't work, an outright embargo might be more effective.

Under the heading of unintended consequences, these measures drove up the cost of foreign goods, which also encouraged smuggling.

The word "mercantilism" was coined after the fact to describe the commercial practices that had been carried on since the 1400s when European explorers began planting not just their country's flag but also their countrymen on foreign shores. The greater the commercial prospects—real or imagined—the greater the attempt to control the commerce.

But giving a name to the trade practices that were in vogue for some 300 years can lead to the impression that there was one mode of conduct applied uniformly by all nations. As one writer described it, "there was nothing logical of consistent about mercantilism, and that it displayed, in fact, enormous variation."

The first mercantilist nation of the era was Portugal. Encouraged by her ruling Prince Henry, known to this day as "Henry the Navigator" for the royal school founded to teach the maritime arts, Portugese traders started pushing down the west coast of Africa in the early 1400s. Their immediate goal was to find a way to import products—including slaves—directly from Africa and the east and cut out the middlemen who were bringing them overland into North Africa and across the Mediterranean Sea.

They were convinced, rightly, that there had to be a southern end to the continent, opening the path north and east to India. In 1488, Bartolomeo Dias found the southern end of Africa, naming it the Cape of Good Hope. Ten years later, Vasco De Gama reached India, opening that subcontinent to exploitation and by 1542 Portuguese traders had extended their explorations all the way to China and Japan.

Nor had the Portugese been less active in their home waters. Starting with the capture of the Moorish city of Ceuta just inside the Straits of Gilbraltar in 1415, by the early 1500s, they had also established their supremacy in the Red Sea and Persian Gulf.

Portugal was not particularly interested in colonization or subjugation. She fought the natives—and later her European competitors—where necessary to protect her trading outposts.

The discovery of the New World by Columbus in 1492 under Spanish sponsorship added a new dimension to the aspirations of both Portugal and Spain. Only two years later, with a papal representative as mediator, a north-south line of demarcation was agreed upon dividing Spanish and Portugese territories. In 1500, the treaty was revised, shifting the line further west, putting what is now Brazil in the Portugese sector, which the Portugese soon exploited.

The eventual Portugese mercantilism took the form of a complete monopoly, controlling the distribution system from its source to the end market.

Neighbors though they might be, Spain's approach took a much different direction. The Portugese were interested in trade, the Spanish in wealth. In a country where two percent of the population owned 90 percent of the wealth, the Spanish grandees considered commerce or production as menial.

Trying to find China and India by heading west, her explorers had instead found something completely new, which they hastened to exploit with great rapacity and success. By the mid 1500s, the Aztec and Inca empires had been overthrown, their treasures plundered and shipped home, their populations put to work in gold and silver mines.

In an effort to control general commerce, Spain closed its colonial ports to any foreign vessel, a special license was required to export to the Spanish colonies and all colonial trade was channeled through Spain.

Spanish explorers soon crossed the Isthmus of Panama, discovered the Pacific Ocean and penetrated into the American Southwest. Pushing into the Pacific, still looking for the Far East, they took possession of the Philippine Islands in 1565.

But by the mid 1500s, things were starting to go bad for both Portugal and Spain. While Portugal's mercantile practices took the form of a monopoly and Spain's the accumulation of wealth, both made the same basic mistake. Neither invested the proceeds of their endeavors in building their infrastructures. They were content rather to buy what they needed—including military forces—from whatever source had them available.

These expenditures enriched the Dutch, French and English and so helped sow the seeds of their eventual undoing. Financed in great part by their business with Portugal and Spain, Dutch shipyards became the greatest in western Europe. The enterprising Dutch also developed a new, more cost-effective class of sailing ship, built for commerce and requiring a much smaller crew.

With its increased navy and merchant fleet, the Dutch began to take over the chain of Portugese trading stations and eventually controlled the links all the way to Japan and China. Like the Portugese and Spanish, the Dutch looked upon the entire structure as a means of supply.

Near the end of the 16th Century, England and France began to emerge as serious competitors to the Dutch and Spanish. Through the second half of the century, they had been growing their navies and soon the Spanish galleons, especially those carrying the annual shipment of gold and silver across the Atlantic, became targets of privateers and so was born the golden age of the Caribbean pirate.

Spain eventually lost her Caribbean islands to the French and English. The Dutch in 1626 established a North American colony after buying Manhattan Island from the Indians for the infamous $24, nestled between English colonies both north and south. It lasted until 1667, when it was ceded to Great Britain after a three-year war. But it was during that same year that the Dutch sailed into British waters, sank five battleships and towed the *Royal Charles* back to Holland.

By the early 1700s, Portugal and Spain had been essentially pushed to the world's sidelines, leaving the oceans to England, France and The Netherlands.

The commercial competition came mainly in the form of their quasi-governmental trading companies—the Dutch East India Company, dating from 1602; the British East India Company, chartered in 1599, and the late-coming French East India Company, founded in 1664. One of the strengths of the Dutch enterprise in the early stages was that it had far fewer trade restrictions than either its predecessors or its contemporaries. Fewer restrictions meant it was open to more shippers to more destinations.

Naturally, when these commercial interests conflicted, armed warfare was frequent. More often than not, it pitted the ambitious British against one of the other three mercantile powers—the Netherlands in the Malay Archipelago, France in India and Spain in the New World.

The Dutch in 1613 attempted the establishment of a colony on the northern coast of South America, but the Spanish wiped it out the next year. In 1623, the Dutch discouraged English incursions into its spice territory in the East Indies by the massacre of British factors at Amboyna. By 1640, after more than a decade of warfare, the Dutch West Indies Company gained control of Brazil's sugar industry, the world's leading exporter.

The Dutch were also financially astute, putting their capital in a wide range of havens. "A third of the capital of the Bank of England in the mid 18th Century belonged to Dutch shareholders."[1]

Eventually, however, it was the ongoing wars with France that wore The Netherlands down, leaving the international stage to the French and English. Given the centuries of political, religious and commercial competition between the two, the outcome was a foregone conclusion. One naturally had to emerge as superior.

But in their mercantilist pursuits, the two held one viewpoint not shared by Portugal, Spain or The Netherlands in that they saw the far-flung outposts with their native population as a market for their goods as well as a source of imports.

It took nearly half a century of nearly continuous wars between Great Britain and France to settle the question. Most noteworthy was the struggle for control of India between the British and French East India Companies. Under the leadership of Robert Clive, who rose from a clerk's post to commander of the British company's armed forces, France's position in the subcontinent was substantially reduced.

Britain had no official territorial ambitions in India in the early 1700s, "but it could not see its East India Company forced out by agents of the French company in collaboration with Indian princes. Naval forces were therefore dispatched to the Indian Ocean and they not only allowed Clive to shift from Madras to Calcutta at will, but gradually cut off the French posts in India from Europe and from each other. By the end of the war (Seven Years War), all the French establishments in India, as in Africa and America, were at the mercy of the British. The French overseas lay prostrate and France itself was again detached from the overseas world upon which much of its economy rested. In 1761, France made an alliance with Spain, which was alarmed for the safety of its own American empire after the British victories at Quebec and in the Caribbean. But the British also defeated Spain."[2]

The seemingly seamless transition from war to war climaxed with the Seven Years War that concluded with the Treaty of Paris in 1763.

To realize the wide range of diversity lumped together under the general "mercantilism" label, it is only necessary to look at the British, whose mercantilism took different courses in different parts of the world.

Irish and Scotch trade was controlled by edict from the Crown or, later, Parliament and both countries were close enough to ensure enforcement, even if it meant armed patrol boats off the Irish coast to intercept contraband cargos.

Britain's trade regulations arguably fell heaviest on the Irish. Nowhere in the Christian world was the heavy hand of English mercantilism so evident over so long a period.

Prohibitions against Irish goods are on record as early as 1339, when Edward III appointed an admiral to stop traffic between Ireland and the continent. It is interesting to note that almost 500 years later (1831) under William IV it was enacted "that a person found in possession of Irish tobacco should suffer a heavy penalty."[3]

By the beginning of the 14th Century, the trade of Ireland with the continent of Europe was important. This condition of things naturally did not suit commercial England. So at an early period she began to stifle Irish industry and trade.

"The Irish woolen manufacturers began to rival England's. So in 1571, Elizabeth imposed restriction on the Irish woolen trade with the Netherlands and other parts of the continent.

"Ireland tried her hand at manufacturing cotton. England met this move with a 25% duty on Irish cotton imported into England. And next forbade the inhabitants of England to wear any cotton other than that of British manufacture.

"Ireland attempted to develop her tobacco industry. But a law against its growth was passed in the first year of Charles the Second.

"Four and five centuries ago and upward, the Irish fisheries were second in importance in Europe. Under careful English nursing they were, a century and a half ago, brought to the vanishing point."[4]

"About the same time, 1715, a heavy emigration started from Ireland, consisting both of Protestants of Scottish ancestry (the so-called Scotch-Irish), and of Catholic Irish from the Ulster counties. Irish farmers found their prosperity threatened, if not ruined, by the British commercial regulations, and the artisans complained about British restrictions on woolen manufactures."[5]

"Even the bitter anti-Irish Froude, in his *English in Ireland* is constrained to confess 'England governed Ireland for what she deemed her own interest, making her calculations on the gross balance of her trade ledgers and leaving her moral obligations aside, as if right and wrong had been blotted out of the statute books of the universe.' "[6]

In India, it was enforced at sword point against both European competitors—notably the French—and the native non-European inhabitants. Because it took a year or more to exchange messages between Europe and India in the 1600s and early 1700s, authority was delegated to the East India Company.

The first English Acts of Navigation came in 1651 under Oliver Cromwell, but they were merely extensions of trade regulations initiated under Elizabeth I almost 100 years earlier. They forbade the importation of goods into England except by English vessels or vessels of the country from which the goods originated. These provisions were aimed primarily at the Dutch, who were at the time Britain's most formidable rival in commercial shipping.

Charles II in 1660 sought to strengthen the early Acts of Navigation by decreeing that certain "enumerated articles" originating in the North America colonies could be exported only to England. Among the earliest enumerated items were tobacco, sugar, wool and molasses.

Three years later, a second Navigation Act forbade the English colonies to trade with other European countries.

European goods bound for the North American colonies had to be unloaded at an English port and reloaded for shipment in an English vessel. The purpose was, of course, to produce income for Britain and the inevitable result was to increase the cost in the colonies.

Still not satisfied, legislation passed by the Parliament in 1672 imposed customs duties on merchandise shipped from one American colony to another.

"For help in enforcing the new trade regulations, Charles II could not place much reliance in the colonial governments. Least of all could he depend on Massachusetts, the worst offender, which dared to behave practically like an independent republic, even usurping the sovereign's prerogative of coining money. The Puritan oligarchs, whose religion in itself was obnoxious to him, persisted in maintaining their own established church instead of the Church of England, thus violating the terms of the Massachusetts Bay Company's charter, which obliged the colony to conform to English law. Many of the Massachusetts merchants, disregarding the Navigation Acts as well, evaded the payment of duties and made smuggling a regular business."[7]

Even those industries not previously restricted came in time to challenge English interests. In the face of a growing woolen industry in the American colonies, the Woolen Act of 1699 prevented any American colony from exporting wool, wool yarn or wool cloth to any place whatsoever. In 1732 there was the Hat Act, whereby beaver fur hats were barred from export from the colonies. The Molasses Act of 1733 was "a supplement to the navigation system, designed to stop the importation of French West Indian molasses into the colonies and to bring larger profits to the sugar planters in the British West Indies."[8]

"The tax on molasses, six pence per gallon, was designed to be prohibitive . . . . the measure was not enforced until after 1758 . . . ." In fact, the "duty of sixpence a gallon on foreign molasses was particularly heavy, amounting to about 100 percent ad valorem." [9]

The act also imposed taxes on imported rum and sugar, but they were incidental in value to that of the molasses for rum making.

It is ironic that France's mercantilist practices made molasses from the French islands cheaper in the North American colonies than that from the British islands. French wine makers lobbied successfully against the distilling of rum, so successfully in fact that molasses was an unwanted byproduct of sugar refining and so was available to Yankee traders at 20 to 40% cheaper than British.

The 1773 tax on tea in the American colonies was related to the Regulating Act of the same year which put Parliament in direct control of India, taking it from the financially troubled East India Company. In return, the company was granted exclusive rights to sell tea direct to the colonies, rather than through a middle man.

In North America, with its basically English population, Westminster attempted to control through fiat. But given the vast geography involved, and the fact that those to whom enforcement was delegated were susceptible to bribery, much of the enforcement was lax. Smuggling was a way of life for many and not particularly frowned on by the general population.

Molasses was an instructive case of the widespread evasion of taxes. Prior to 1758, Knollenberg notes that the going rate in Boston was about a tenth of the tax, in Salem about half-pence a gallon and in New York one-quarter to one-half pence per gallon. Prior to 1760, revenues from molasses never amounted to as much as £1,000 a year and was often less than £100.

"The magnitude of the indulged trade in foreign molasses," Knollenberg continues, "is indicated by the amount entered for duty from 1767 to 1771, after the rate of duty had been reduced to a penny a gallon, totaled over 3 million gallons a year."[10]

For some 150 years, the American colonies had been relatively isolated from the mother country and for some 40 years prior to the Seven Years War had been the beneficiary of her "salutary neglect," all of which allowed the growth of a practical working arrangement within the colonies that didn't necessarily match what London had in mind.

"They (settlers in America) lived as though on another planet, and this was their dearest wish."[11]

That period came to an end in 1742, when Robert Walpole resigned as prime minister after losing control of a majority in the House of Commons. Walpole had declined to interfere with the North American colonies in the belief that the larger their commerce was allowed to grow—even at the expense of conformity to the letter of English law—the heavier would be their demand for English goods.

So while he restricted colonial trade through measures like the Molasses Act, a prohibition on copper smelting and the Hat Act, he refused to try to tax the colonies.

"The navigation acts, originally designed to transfer the monopoly of the carrying trade from Dutch to English bottoms and to control the market for colonial products, seemed justified by the vast increase in the volume of commerce. During the reign of George II, exports had nearly doubled and between 1760 and 1774, notwithstanding an unwise change in colonial policy, they grew from £14,693,270 to £17,128,029."[12]

But following the Treaty of Paris, George III, supported by an increasingly captive Parliament, undertook a series of measures that intruded into the colonial way of life. In the length of time it takes an infant to become a teenager, the history of the English-speaking world was changed forever.

Chapter 2

To understand the variety of currents at work in the colonies, it is also necessary to take a step back and look at one the three major threads of our history—religion—and how the ebb and flow of religious thought in England made their effects felt in North America.

One might say it all came about because of two unhappy people—one a Catholic priest and the other the king of England. Together, they sowed the seeds for the panoply of Christian faiths we see today.

The roots of religious separatism can be conveniently dated from 1517 when the priest—Martin Luther—posted his declarations on the Wittenberg castle door, beginning a schism in the Catholic church which had been for centuries the unquestioned and unquestionable voice in ecclesiastic matters for all of Western Europe.

Henry VIII ascended the throne of Catholic England in 1509, but by the 1530s Luther's ideas had been circulating in England as well as in continental Europe for almost a quarter of a century. They had taken hold in many quarters. In France, while there had been no open revolt against the church, there were many who were sympathetic to Luther's views.

Just before Henry's split with Rome, Swiss theologian John Calvin underwent a self-described "sudden conversion" against Catholicism but, before long, also fell out with the Lutherans, "which ended in the separation of the evangelical party into the two great sections of Lutherans and Reformed."[1]

Calvinism was to take root in Scotland and is later reflected in Puritan England and the New England colonies.

When the Vatican barred Henry from divorcing Catherine of Aragon in 1534, Henry proclaimed the Anglican Church the official, established church of England with himself as its head. Needless to say, the Anglican Church recognized divorce and Henry was rid of his widowed sister-in-law turned wife.

While the religious split cleared the way for five more royal marriages, more importantly it set England on a 160-year zig-zag course between Catholicism and various stripes of Protestantism. The impact on the course of the kingdom cannot be overlooked or underrated. Religion became during that time a matter of life and death since both sides—when they were in power—felt they were doing God's work in eliminating the other side.

In matters of faith, just because the king says it's so doesn't necessarily make it so, even if Henry attempted to impose the Anglican Church on the populace with a very heavy hand. There were still many in England who clung to the Catholic faith while in Scotland the Calvinists saw the Anglican church as thinly veiled Catholicism, with Henry in place of the Pope.

The official shift away from Catholicism combined with the long-standing competition with France combined to raise the specter of Catholic Ireland becoming a back door through which the French might try to put England in a vise east and west. And there were some grounds for that fear, since in later years efforts were in fact made to use Ireland as a staging ground for invasion.

While the English had been resident in Ireland for some 400 years—years in which they looked down on the Irish as relatively uncivilized barbarians—at least they were co-religionists. Trade and commerce were the major points of difference between them.

To ensure control over the island, Henry began sending Anglican "colonists" with the open intent of exerting control over the island.

In some cases, the island also became haven for non-conforming Protestants seeking a place where they could worship as they chose. While this might not have set too well with the Anglicans, it was even less welcome by the native Catholics.

Henry VIII was succeeded on his death in 1567 by his nine-year-old son, Edward VI, who reigned only six years and died at 15.

His half-sister, Mary I, came to the throne, and bringing with her the Catholic religion. In short order earned the name "Bloody Mary" for the fervor with which she persecuted Protestants. Over a three-year period, it is estimated that she sent some 200 "heretics" to the stake.

At 37 when she ascended to the throne, Mary was "a strong-willed Tudor who had suffered 20 years of humiliation and ill-treatment for loyalty to her mother and to Catholicism."[2] She was also "the classic image of the old maid, a stiff, sour, plain, hostile, unwanted woman."[3]

The first blood of her reign had already been shed before she was officially seated on the throne. In a maneuver to keep the crown in Protestant hands, Henry's niece, 16-year-old Lady Jane Grey was declared queen. She reigned for nine days and went in short order to the Tower and then the block.

Mary, one year into her reign, married Philip, son of the Catholic Emperor Charles V and even went so far as to reconcile with Rome with Cardinal Pole installed as Archbishop of Canterbury. These events eroded with store of good will she had with the people at the start of her reign and even resulted in an ill-fated rebellion. Her revival of the anti-heresy laws that resulted in the bonfires that consumed "heretics" further eroded her popular support.

The crowning insult to Mary's short reign was the war with France through her alliance with the Hapsburg Empire. Early in 1558, Calais—England's last toehold on the continent—fell to the French after centuries of English possession. Mary died late in the same year and Cardinal Pole only a few hours later.

According to London undertaker Henry Machyn's diary "all the churches in London did ring, and at night (men) did make bonfires and set tables in the street, and did eat and drink; and make merry, for the new queen."[4]

Only five years after gaining the throne, Mary was succeeded her younger half-sister, Protestant Elizabeth I, daughter of the ill-fated Anne Boleyn. During her 45-year reign, there was at least relative peaceful coexistence between the official Anglican Church, the Catholics and Presbyterians. Rome didn't take a positive view of her reign, particularly when it came to her further efforts to "colonize" Ireland. She was excommunicated in 1570, an action that she apparently shrugged off as unimportant. However, the excommunication in effect branded the queen a heretic and absolved Catholics of the any allegiance to her. Caught between the requirements of legislation passed by the Protestant Parliament and the influx of extremist Catholic clergy, the stakes were erected once more and some 250 Catholics suffered imprisonment or death.

A co-equal threat to religion in the queen's view were the Puritans, who had an advantage over the Catholics. While the Catholics were barred from political office, the Puritans worked within Parliament to change the laws. Elizabeth, however, vetoed those efforts as usurping her royal prerogative. Eventually, the Puritans were forced to find themselves a place outside the Anglican Church.

The situation on the religious front began to come apart early in the 17th Century when James I, already James VI of Scotland, ascended to the throne in 1603. James was son of the Catholic "Bloody Mary" but had been brought up in the Scottish Presbyterian Church, so both adherents were expecting sympathetic treatment. Both were to be disappointed.

The Catholics were more openly disappointed than the Calvinists. Only two years into his reign, a plot was concocted to blow up Parliament buildings when James I would be in attendance. Happily, at least for James, the plot was discovered and to this day the English celebrate Guy Fawkes Day, named for one of the principals in the plot.

On James' death in 1625, his son became king as Charles I and he was less politically savvy than his father. He was married to the Catholic Henrietta Maria, sister of France's King Louis XIII, but still head of the official Anglican Church. He made the fatal mistake of trying to impose the Anglican Church, with all its formal trappings, on the Scotch Presbyterians. Their suspicion of Charles wasn't lessened by the fact that he had a Catholic queen. His edict also named the king head of the combined Anglican-Presbyterian church—a provision the Scots were not about to accept—which made the question political as well as religious.

The standoff devolved into a four-year civil war that pitted the king's "cavaliers" against the Protestant "roundheads," under the leadership of Oliver Cromwell. After unsuccessfully soliciting an Irish Catholic army to augment his forces, Charles eventually surrendered to the Scottish, who in turn, sold him to the English.

Cromwell, protector of the proclaimed English Commonwealth, resolved the impasse of a deposed monarch in 1649 with fatal results for Charles, despite warnings of reprisals from Louis XIV of France.

After some eight years of insurrection in Ireland, Cromwell turned his New Model Army loose to suppress rebellions in Ireland between 1649 and 1650. The long delay was prompted by discord at home but action was finally precipitated by rumors that Charles II, then in exile in France, planned to go to Ireland to raise an army to invade England.

It is estimated that Cromwell's forces slaughtered more than 40 percent of the Irish population—most notably the massacre of some 3,500 soldiers and civilians at Drogheda and another 2,000 soldiers at Wexford a month later—and the remainder were exiled to County Connaught in 1653. Between 1650 and 1651, the rebellious Scotch Presbyterians who fought for a Stuart restoration in the person of Charles II were likewise defeated.

Staunch Protestant that he might have been, there was a practical side to Cromwell that twisted the threads of religion together with those of mercantilism. He allied with the Catholic French in 1657—who were, incidentally, persecuting Protestants in their country—against the equally Catholic Spanish and acquiesced in a war with England's perennial commercial opponent, the Protestant Dutch.

The Protestant Commonwealth of Cromwell lasted 10 years, but began showing cracks after some five years, thanks to Cromwell's authoritarian, one-man rule. Cromwell disbanded the so-called Rump Parliament in 1653, clearing the hall at swordpoint in what was no more than a coup d'etat. It was succeeded by an appointed "Barebones Parliament" and protector became despot. It was as close to a theocratic government England was to see. The Commonwealth collapsed on his death and a brief attempt to continue it by his son. Within two years of his death, Cromwell's corpse was exhumed for the purpose of decorating the gibbet at Tyburn.

After 10 years of the Protector, the English were more than ready to welcome the return of royalty in the person of Charles II, perhaps more ready than Charles was to occupy the throne. He had spent years in exile and returned to

England unable to trust the Anglicans, Catholics or Presbyterians. It was during his reign that the Test Act to ensure only Protestant successors was passed by Parliament.

Charles died in 1685 and was succeeded by his younger brother as James II. Unlike his brother, he was rigid, dour and Catholic. He flatfootedly refused to take the Test Act oath. Nor did he gain any approval of the populace for his brother's deathbed conversion to Catholicism, which, it was widely believed, he had arranged by smuggling a priest into the king's bedchamber.

James II became even bolder, appointing Catholics to major positions in the army, engineering the repeal of various anti-Catholic measures and clearing the way for them to hold political positions of power. During his first year on the throne, he prorogued Parliament and it never met again during the remainder of his reign.

The four years of James II's reign was as unsettled politically and religiously as any of his predecessors. He compounded stupidity with obstinacy. After the death of his first wife, he married an Italian Catholic princess and, on the birth of his son, had only Catholic witnesses to the birth. Naturally, Anglican opponents charged subterfuge, alleging the baby had been smuggled into the room in a bedpan by a nurse.

Faced with a practicing and unrepentant Catholic as king and head of the Anglican Church and now with a male heir to carry on, English Protestants of all stripes were at their wits end.

Feelers went across the English Channel to Charles' Protestant daughter Mary by his first wife and her husband, William III of Orange, Europe's premier champion of Protestantism. They offered her the crown if she and William would only come and rescue the country from James and his Catholic issue.

Assured of a warm welcome, William mounted an invasion in 1688 and, faced with the prospect of hostilities,

James' supporters melted into the woodwork. Return of the throne to Protestant hands has come to be known in history as the Glorious Revolution since it was prompted by the English themselves.

James' last effort to regain his crown came about two years after William and Mary's accession when, with the support of France, he landed in Ireland to raise an army among Catholic supporters in Ireland. He set up a royal court complete with diplomatic representatives from Louis XIV's court. But thanks to James' treatment of the French diplomats and military advisors, the French began to cool to the whole invasion idea, particularly in view of the growing resentment of the French among the Irish.

The decisive encounter was along the banks of the Boyne River near Dublin and only four miles from Drogheda on July 1, 1690. William's forces, supplemented by Danish mercenaries and Dutch regiments, had a numerical advantage of about 10,000, some 36,000 to James' 25,000. They also had a huge advantage in artillery, which they exerted in a day and night of cannonade that preceded the battle itself. Considering the number of combatants, casualties were low—some 1,500 of James' troops and 500 of the English.

The Protestant Orange Order in Ulster still celebrate the anniversary of the battle, although history makes little mention of a significant presence of the Protestant Irish in the battle.

James was in due course captured, but William had no great desire to send his father-in-law to the block, so he arranged that James should escape. Which he did within the month and, as expected, followed his wife and child into exile in France.

Mary was reluctant to become sole ruler of England and William did not fancy the role of prince consort. As a result, a joint regency was established and their reign is the only one in English history to bear a double identity—William and Mary it was and William and Mary it still is.

With its last Catholic defender in England vanquished, Ireland's native population faced the "Protestant Ascendency" and the anti-Catholic legislation that went with it.

Each swing of the religious pendulum from Henry VIII in 1534 to the accession of William and Mary took its toll in human life and created its own migration. In some cases, the migrants were believers fleeing persecution and in others they were encouraged to relocate to the detriment of the native population.

Religion was very much a matter of life and death and the journey to unknown lands in North America was sometimes more preferable to what was faced at home.

These tides were augmented by those who crossed the Atlantic with more commercial interests in mind, such as the settlers in Virginia.

In 1701, Parliament passed the Act of Settlement that once again decreed only Protestant successors. This time, the act was not overturned and it led the way for the Hanoverian line of Georges.

Chapter 3

From today's viewpoint, there might not seem to be a big gap between 1606, when the first English colony appeared, and George's coronation in 1763, but it is after all 157 years, about the same period of time that separates the Civil War from the new millennium. And in any age, 157 years is a long time in which to develop customs, even societies, particularly when separated by 3,000 miles in distance and two to three months in time from a government that is paying scant attention, thanks to its problems at home.

By the accession of George III there was a string of 13 English colonies up and down the Eastern seaboard established under five different monarchs with an estimated population of two million, including sizable numbers of other nationalities.

Over those years, these 13 colonies had undergone an historic transformation. Through the first 60 or so years, there were virtually isolated dots along the seaboard with little to tie one another together except their connection to a common homeland—which they felt with varying degrees of affection—and a certain degree of inter-colony commerce.

Over the next two generations, however, the population increased almost sevenfold. A network of roads began connecting the growing number of settlements, a score of newspapers appeared along with a rudimentary postal service. Domestic agriculture and commerce both benefited from and stimulated continual expansion.

These avenues also were the means to transport something else from settlement to settlement—ideas. Granted that in 1763 the colonies were far from united, but they were at least beginning to feel a common sense that they were something more than Englishmen in a strange land.

Howard[1] asserts that "Founded at different times, under separate charters, and for diverse motives, the American provinces were in fact 13 distinct societies. Except for their allegiance to a common sovereign, they were in theory as independent as if they were foreign states."

While Howard's contention might be true up until the late 1600s, by the time of George III the idea that they were separate and distinct societies is not necessarily true, especially as regards the New England colonies, where there was a strong—but not always amicable—interrelationship.

Before looking at a brief history of the individual colonies, a word of caution. Geographic names in North America in the 1600s had a way of evolving into their modern definitions. Virginia then was a loose term meaning much of the Atlantic seaboard and even included Bermuda after 1612. Maryland was also part of "Virginia" while the Plymouth Company grant included Maine.

England's first attempt to colonize North America, the ill-fated Roanoke colony, disappeared and why is still is a source of conjecture.

The first viable English colony in North America was Jamestown, a colony established by the London Company in Virginia (or the South Virginia Company, Virginia Company of London, the London Company or simply, the Virginia

Company), in 1607 under charter from James I and named in honor of Elizabeth I, the "Virgin Queen" whose reign covered the seven decades from 1533 to 1603.

At the same time, a charter was issued to the North Virginia Company or Plymouth Company. Each was granted 100 square miles with the proviso that they not settle within 100 miles of one another.

As something of a coincidence, both Virginia and Massachusetts were founded where they were through the vagaries of the weather. The Virginia colonists had planned to settle around Roanoke Island in what was to become the Carolinas, but were blown off course and ended in Jamestown. The original Plymouth settlers had been heading much further south but inclement sailing weather fetched them up on the Massachusetts coast.

In its first years, the Virginia colony was held together by Captain John Smith and was increased through the addition of 400 new settlers about 1610 under Thomas West, Lord Delaware (or "de la Warr").

In the aftermath of an internal struggle for control of the Virginia Company, James I put an end to the colony's representative assembly in 1624, only five years after its first meeting, revoked the colony's charter and Virginia became a royal colony, the first of many similar revocations over the next 125 years.

Not ones to be left behind, the Dutch hired an Englishman by the name of Henry Hudson to take a look at North America and its commercial potential. By 1609, he was exploring the river that bears his name for the Dutch United East India Company and by 1613 Dutch settlements were appearing.

While the Dutch are primarily associated with Manhattan, which they bought from the Indians in 1626 for the infamous $24 in beads and baubles and named New Amsterdam, they spread out over a considerable distance while other English colonies sprang up around them. As always, with commercial prospects in mind, they extended into what is now New Jersey and Connecticut. Inevitably, once the English had grown to sufficient strength, this would lead to conflict between the outposts that reflected the long-standing rivalry between their mother countries.

Just 14 years after Jamestown and seven years after the first Dutch settlements, the English Plymouth colony was founded far to the north on the shores of what was to become Massachusetts Bay. Ostensibly, they were traveling from England with commercial interests in mind, but when the Pilgrims set foot on Plymouth Rock they were really there for religious reasons.

Despite the name, it should be noted that the Pilgrims were traveling under license from the Virginia Company, not the Plymouth Company, and were bound for the area at the mouth of the Hudson River. Because of the lateness of the season—they arrived in early winter—it was decided to remain where they were rather than travel further south.

Pilgrims, unlike the Puritans who were to follow them to New England 10 years later, were Protestant "separatists," seeking to separate themselves from the Anglican established church of England. It has been suggested that since religious Dissenters were some of the ruling monarch's less desirable citizens during this prolonged period of exodus, they were granted less desirable settlement rights in the New World.

In the same year that the Pilgrims made landfall, Sir Frederick Gorges and others applied for and received a new royal charter to replace the relatively inactive Plymouth Company (or North Virginia Company) under the name Council for New England. It was granted the land between the 40th and 48th degrees latitude, in effect all of the land from south of New York city to the northern tip of Maine.

From these holdings, the council made a variety of land grants, some of which were conflicting.

In 1628 the council granted to the Governor and Company of Massachusetts Bay in New England land extending from three miles south of the mouth of the Charles River to three miles north of the Merrimac. Convinced that a royal charter was preferable to a land grant, the Massachusetts Bay Colony asked and, in 1629, received a royal charter from King Charles I.

The charter consolidated the settlements in Maine, New Hampshire and Massachusetts with the exception of Plymouth Colony. That was to come later.

Between 1630 and 1640, the colony saw tremendous growth, with some 20,000 making the Atlantic crossing. It has been called the largest migration of Europeans since the Crusades.

Among these émigrés in 1631 was a young English preacher by the name of Roger Williams, whose preaching stirred opposition in Boston, Salem and Plymouth. Although ordered out of the colony, he persisted. The colony decided to deport him, but before they could execute the order he and a band of followers escaped southward. Once clear of the colony's borders, they put down roots in a town they named Providence, sowing the seeds for Rhode Island in 1636. Williams' teachings were to provide the foundation for the Baptist beliefs, which among other things include separation of church and state.

He was joined in 1638 by Anne Hutchinson, who was also exiled from Massachusetts after being tried and found guilty of sedition for holding religious meetings for women at which she espoused a doctrine contrary to Puritan beliefs. She brought with her husband and 14 children to found Pocasset (Portsmouth).

Like Williams and Hutchinson, most Rhode Island settlers were refuges from the Puritan theology, law and custom. Because of their spirit of freedom, Rhode Island for many years was "the most turbulent of all the New England colonies."

Williams obtained a charter of incorporation in 1643 or 1644 from a committee of the Parliament, since at the time

Charles I and Parliament were not on speaking terms, but it included no land grant.

Following the restoration, a new charter issued by Charles II in 1663 for "Rhode Island and Providence Plantations" granted religious freedom. However, state legislature barred Catholics from the rights of freemen. The colony was never popular with its neighbors and was excluded from the New England Confederation of 1643.

Religious disagreement with the Massachusetts theocracy also led to the formation of Connecticut. Preacher Thomas Hooker arrived in Boston in 1632 on the same ship as Cotton Mather. While Mather became the preeminent Puritan pastor in Boston, Hooker ended up in neighboring Newtown (now Cambridge). He disagreed with Gov. Winthrop over limiting suffrage to church members. In June, 1636, he and his congregation migrated to the Connecticut River valley and founded Hartford. Congregations from Dorchester and Watertown followed, founding Windsor and Wethersfield. The government was provisional for a year under Massachusetts. Meeting in Hartford, representatives of the three towns produced the first written constitution that really created a government. There was no religious test for citizenship and no mention made of allegiance to the king. Of all the colonies, its government was most like that of today. New Haven in 1638 became genesis of New Haven Colony that included Milford, Guilford and Stamford.

The Dutch of New Amsterdam, however, claimed Connecticut River Valley. Ensuing hostilities with the Dutch and with the Pequot Indians eventually drove the English out.

After occupying the land for some 30 years without any claim except that derived from the Indians, a charter was obtained from Charles II in 1662 as a corporate colony. One of Charles' motives is reputed to be the creation of rivalries to Massachusetts.

Granting of the charter led some New Haven residents to migrate to New Jersey rather than become part of

Connecticut. John Winthrop, son of a Massachusetts governor, was governor for many years.

Massachusetts also played a continuing role in the development at the northern end of New England.

In 1622, the Council for New England granted Gorges and John Mason the land between the Merrimac and Sagadahock (now Kennebec) Rivers, essentially today's New Hampshire, Vermont and Maine.

Efforts to lure settlers to the area were not notably successful, although there were several small settlements, many bolstered by emigrants from Massachusetts.

By 1629, Gorges and Mason decided to divide their holdings, with Mason retaining what was to become New Hampshire, and Gorges Maine. Both holdings were also claimed by Massachusetts, sparking a prolonged legal battle in England, particularly as regarded Maine. After Gorges' death in 1647, several of the towns decided to become part of Massachusetts as Gorges' heirs continued their dispute. Finally, in 1664, a court ruled in favor of the heirs, returning the property to the Gorges family. The matter was finally resolved in 1677, when Massachusetts bought out the family for £1,250. The area never became a separate colony, but continued as the District of Maine for nearly 150 years until 1820, when it was admitted to the Union as a state.

The history of New Hampshire is hardly less convoluted. Once again, the question was one of conflicting claims between the original grant recipient, Mason, and Massachusetts. These claims were further complicated by the vacillations of succeeding monarchies in England.

Even before the settlements in Maine elected to become part of Massachusetts, New Hampshire settlements came to that conclusion in 1641. By 1679, Charles II—in part because of the ongoing Gorges litigation—had come to the conclusion that Massachusetts was becoming too independent for his liking and separated New Hampshire into a separate colony. Under

James II, the two colonies were reunited, only to be separated for the last time in 1691 under William and Mary. However, the New Hampshire governor was, in effect, a lieutenant governor under the governor of Massachusetts. It wasn't until 1749, about a century later, that the claims of the Mason heirs were finally purchased.

While the New England colonies were sorting out their various territorial boundaries, there were troubles a couple of hundred miles to their south with the Dutch.

As previously mentioned, the Dutch East (Annals of America) India Company had sent Henry Hudson to explore the Atlantic coast in 1609 and the first Dutch colonies were established at the mouth of the river named for him in 1613. Given their economic rivalry worldwide, a Dutch settlement situated between the northern and southern English colonies could well be expected to cause trouble—and it did. As the New England colonies spread southward and the Dutch expanded into New Jersey and Connecticut, friction was inevitable.

For so long as New Amsterdam lasted, its government was autocratic and aristocratic. Under its charter of "privileges and exemptions" adopted in 1629, any member of the West (Elson) India Company who could bring at least 50 settlers over the age of 15 was granted an estate of 16 miles frontage on a bay or river or eight miles on both sides of a river. Owners of these grants—potroons—soon controlled a vast expanse of the Hudson River Valley. Hereditary ownership of these tracts continued well into the 1800s.

Between 1633 and 1636 there are clashes in Connecticut as the Dutch lay claim to the Connecticut River valley and in 1637 a company of Dutch, in the employ of the King of Sweden, organize the New Sweden Company for Swedish settlers in Delaware over the protests of some of the Dutch and founded Christina (Wilmington).

Some of the monopolistic restrictions on trade and farming were relaxed in the early 1640s, due in some part to the relative freedoms the Dutch citizens observed in the surrounding English settlements and granted in the English towns under their jurisdiction, and the New Amsterdam began to assume a cosmopolitan atmosphere.

Relations between England and The Netherlands began to change in 1648 with the Peace of Utrecht that ended the Thirty Years War, a war in which they were allied against France. With the French vanquished, the Dutch began to exert their commercial muscle on the high seas and overseas. With the Commonwealth ending the English civil war and Oliver Cromwell's assumption of power in 1650, England adopted its first Acts of Navigation which were directed primarily against the Dutch.

Coupled with this heightened economic warfare, New Amsterdam was treated to an unfortunate collection of governors that doomed New Amsterdam to a continuous succession of quarrels—with the English in Connecticut, the Swedes in Delaware and the Indians everywhere. Despite changes in the company's rules issued from The Netherlands, Peter Stuyvesant, the last Dutch governor, ruled for a decade without an elected assembly.

In 1655, the Dutch trading company took over New Sweden, ending any concerted Swedish effort to cut out a national foothold in the New World.

After the English monarchy was restored in 1660, it all came to an end in 1664, when the English won the Second Anglo-Dutch War and evicted the Dutch from all their holdings. Charles II granted the colony to his brother, James, Duke of York, and New Amsterdam surrendered without bloodshed and became New York. At the same time, New Jersey was separated from New York and granted a proprietary charter.

Nine years later, in the Third Anglo-Dutch War, the Dutch briefly recaptured New Jersey but ceded it back to England in the following year, ending the Dutch aspirations in North America.

When James, Duke of York, became James II on the death of his brother in 1685, New York's charter was converted from proprietary to royal. The elected assembly was disbanded and Edmund Andros was sent as governor of New York, New England and New Jersey. But even that did not last long, as James II was overthrown by William and Mary and Andros was imprisoned. For two years, New York was ruled by the militia led by Jacob Leisler and his son-in-law, Milborne. It was during that time that the first mass meeting of representatives from the various colonies was held in New York. Order was restored in 1691 by the new governor, Henry Slougher, but Leisler and Milborne were both hanged.

By 1750, the city's population had grown to some 12,000, up from the 1,500 at the time of New Amsterdam's surrender.

Even as Massachusetts Bay Colony was the progenitor of several New England colonies, the New Amsterdam Dutch figured in the history not only of Connecticut but also Delaware and New Jersey, both of which became individual English colonies in 1664.

Delaware joins New York as the only two or the original 13 colonies to be founded by non-English. It also had more claimants in its early days than any other.

The Dutch originally claimed it by right of discovery as they spread out from New Amsterdam about 1631 and placed a small settlement on Delaware Bay near Lewes, but the Indians massacred the settlement.

Sweden's King Gustavus Adolphus incorporated the New Sweden Company in 1627 to establish a settlement on the banks of the Delaware River but, thanks to the Thirty Years War and the king's death, these plans were delayed until 1638. Led by former New Amsterdam governor Peter Minuit, now in the pay of Sweden, the first contingent of settlers built a fort on the site of Wilmington, which they named Christina in honor of their child queen. A second settlement was established at the site of Philadelphia.

After a number of confrontations with the Dutch stretching over 17 years, New Amsterdam governor Peter Stuyvesant sent a fleet to take over New Sweden, ending the Swedish claims in the New World, although the 700 Swedish settlers were permitted to retain their farms.

When New Amsterdam fell to the Duke of York in 1664, Delaware was part of the deal. But in 1682, with the founding of Pennsylvania, the duke sold the property to William Penn and it became that colony's "Lower Three Counties" or the "Territories." In 1702, Penn granted the area its own legislature, but it remained essentially a satellite of Pennsylvania until the revolution.

As noted, New Jersey was part of the grant made by Charles II along with New York to his brother James, Duke of York, after the Dutch were defeated in 1664. James, in turn, handed over the province in the same year to two friends, Lord Berkeley and Sir George Carteret, and it was named in Carteret's former position as governor of the Island of Jersey in the English Channel.

The first emigrants arrived the following year and settled at Elizabethtown, named in honor of Carteret's wife. Even more settlers came overland from New England, particularly from the settlement of New Haven in protest over that town's forced union with Connecticut.

Through the early years, matters were somewhat chaotic. There was a rebellion when the quitrents came due after five years, resulting in the election of an illegal assembly, a temporary recapture of the colony by the Dutch in 1673 and finally the sale of his share by Berkeley to two Quakers, John Fenwick and Edward Byllynge. Byllynge went bankrupt and his share went into the hands of trustees, the most prominent of the group being William Penn.

Like the Maine province, New Jersey was separated in two in 1676, with East Jersey being retained by Carteret and West Jersey by the trustees. Needless to say, the code of laws established in the two Jerseys were far different, with Puritan codes in East Jersey and the far more tolerant Quaker laws in West Jersey.

Before the decade was over, New York governor Edmund Andros claimed jurisdiction over the Jerseys but East Jersey governor Philip Carteret arrested and imprisoned Andros, putting an end to the claim. Two years after George Carteret's death in 1680, East Jersey was sold to a group of 12, including William Penn. Each of these 12 sold half his share, making a 24-member proprietorship and Quaker Robert Barclay was elected governor for life.

With the accession of James, Duke of York, to the throne as James II in 1685 matters changed. James revoked the charters of both Jerseys, combined them with New York and New England and installed Andros as governor over the whole territory.

When James was thrown out on his royal ear by William and Mary four years later, the question of ownership was thrown into a turmoil for years thanks to conflicting claims of the Cartret heirs, of the Quakers and of New York. Queen Anne, in the final year of her reign (1702), made New Jersey a royal colony under the jurisdiction of New York's governor. George II finally separated the colonies in 1732.

Meanwhile, further south, colonies were also growing. In 1628, Charles I had granted the region between Virginia, which by then had acquired a more geographically focused definition, and Spanish Florida to Sir Robert Heath. The area was named Carolina in honor of the king, but early settlement efforts were essentially fruitless.

In 1632, George Calvert (later Lord Baltimore) applied for a royal grant to establish a colony in a section of Virginia that he named Maryland, in honor of Queen Henrietta Maria, the royal consort. Only months after the original Lord Baltimore's death, the patent was granted Cecilius Calvert, the second Lord Baltimore, and settlers began arriving in Virginia in 1634. They traveled on to a settlement they named St. Mary's. As might be surmised from its salute to a Catholic queen, it was the first English colony in North America to grant religious tolerance to Catholics. It lasted about 20 years. Inspired by the English revolution, the Protestant majority repealed the Toleration Act and denied protection of Catholics, although that protection was later restored.

When the revolt spread in England that led to the overthrow of the Catholic James II in 1685, what started in Maryland as a revolt against the proprietary form of government became once again a Protestant-Catholic conflict. After the Protestant William and Mary came to the throne, Maryland's Catholic governor was forced from office, the Protestant Association petitioned the new monarchs to take over the colony. It took a couple of years, but in 1692 Maryland became a royal colony. Catholics were allowed to retain their property rights, but in 1694 the capital was moved from Catholic St. Mary's to Protestant Annapolis.

Sandwiched in between the chartering of Connecticut in 1662 and the acquisition of New York, New Jersey and Delaware from the Dutch in 1664 was Charles II's granting of a charter to a group of eight aristocrat proprietors, principal among them Sir Anthony Ashley Cooper, later the Earl of Shaftesbury, and Sir William Berkeley, governor of Virginia. French explorers 100 years earlier had named the area Carolina in honor of Charles IX of France. Since the current English monarch was also a Charles, the name was retained. Two years after the original charter, it was expanded to include virtually all the area south of Virginia and extending westward "to the South Sea."

There had been some attempt at settling the land, including a settlement of Virginia colonists about 1653 on the banks of the Chowan and Roanoke Rivers in a district called Albermarle after the duke of the same name that comprised the northern portion of the Carolinas. A few years later, some New Englanders tried setting up a town on the Cape Fear River in a district called Clarendon, but that effort was short-lived.

Being aristocrats, the original proprietors tried to import the English form of government into the colony under something called the Grand Model, supposedly concocted by Shaftesbury and John Locke, whose philosophy was to figure so large in Revolutionary times.

Under the plan, the territory was to be divided into counties, each with an earl and two barons, who would own one-fifth of the county. Another fifth would go to the proprietors and the remaining three-fifths to the people as tenants, whose condition would be essentially the same as serfs in England.

One of the problems with the idea was that many of those settlers already there were there to get away from what they felt were restrictive governments further north. They retreated further into the western wilderness. The Grand Model proved impossible to enforce and, after some 20 years of trying, it was abandoned.

Berkeley appointed a Scotch Presbyterian minister named William Drummond as governor of the Albermarle district. His choice proved unfortunate, both for Berkeley and Drummond. The preacher proved sympathetic to Nathaniel Bacon, who led a two-year uprising in Virginia against Berkeley's inability, or unwillingness, to protect the western settlers from the Indians. Bacon died of the fever in 1676 and Drummond the same year on Berkeley's order.

The years between 1677 and 1695 were tumultuous with rapacious governors and another insurrection that held the government for two years between 1678 and 1680. Part of the problem lay in one of the laws adopted by the assembly to attract settlers. It provided that newcomers were exempt from taxes for a year, outlawed any debts incurred outside the district and barred anyone from being sued for any cause arising outside the colony for a period of five years. As might have been predicted, the district became a haven for debtors and others under threat of legal action, earning it the Virginia nickname of "Rogue's Harbor."

Such leniency failed to attract the more stable settler and by 1693, the population was half what it had been 15 years earlier. The Clarendon colony on Cape Fear had been abandoned.

Further south, three shiploads of English immigrants from the island of Barbados pitched their tents in 1670 to form the first settlement along the Ashley River. The following year, Sir John Yeamans joined the colony, bringing with him about 200 slaves. Later the same year, the colony was bolstered by two shiploads of Dutch immigrants from New York.

The settlement labored along for 10 years until the settlers decided on a better location, a point where, later Carolinians were to assert, the Ashley and Cooper Rivers join to form the Atlantic Ocean. Their city was christened Charleston.

With essentially only two principal settlements in the colony about 100 miles apart, by the 1690s they were being referred to as North and South Carolina. Governance of the two colonies was united in 1695, bringing a certain degree of peace and prosperity

Beginning in the mid 1680s, the Carolinas were among the points of destination for hundreds of thousands of Huguenots, French Protestants who fled their country after Louis XIV revoked the 90-year-old Edict of Nantes that had granted them freedom of religion.

The Carolinas also attracted a sizable German community and a variety of other dissenters, including Quakers, which led to internal political problems in the early 1700s. Sir Nathaniel Johnson became governor of the Carolinas in 1703 and one of the first acts passed barred all dissenters from seats in the assembly. This led to a prolonged battle back in England as the dissenters appealed unsuccessfully to the proprietors but successfully to the House of Lords. Faced with the possible loss of their charter by Queen Anne, the proprietors relented, although the Church of England was installed as the official church of the colony.

But even more serious problems were at hand. A combined French and Spanish naval assault on Charleston, a vestige of Queen Anne's War in Europe, was repelled but to the south a combination of Indian tribes waged war along the frontier. In debt to the English colonists and still aggrieved over the number of Indians captured and sold into slavery, it didn't take much agitation from the Spanish to trigger the outbreak. The war lasted about 10 months before the Indians were defeated and scattered, some south into Florida and others migrating as far north as New York.

Wars have a way of increasing debt, and the Indians war in the Carolinas was no exception. But when the assembly asked the proprietors back in England for either direct financial aid or permission to find new sources of revenue through taxes, they were refused. Exasperated, they appealed to the Crown to revoke the charter. In 1719, George I granted their request but it was another 10 years before all the proprietors sold their interests to the crown and North and South Carolina became separate colonies in fact as well as in name.

While debts are usually bad news, they can be an asset if you lend the money to the right people. This was the situation in the case of Pennsylvania. It seems that Admiral Sir William Penn, having served both Cromwell and Charles II, had loaned Charles some £16,000 and after his father's death the younger Penn inherited the debt. He knew what he wanted to do with it, provided he could collect.

Penn had become an adherent of George Fox, who over the past 40 years had drawn some 70,000 others to his religious belief as Quakers. Because they refused to recognize social ranks, pay taxes or wage war, they were less than popular in aristocratic England. At one point, they were described in an act of Parliament as a "mischievous and dangerous people."

Penn in 1680 applied to the king for a grant in the New World which he intended as a haven for the persecuted

Quakers. Perhaps seeing this as a way to cancel his debt and at the same time rid the island of some "mischievous and dangerous people," Charles II the following year granted Penn some 40,000 square miles from the northern border of Maryland northward "as far as plantable, which is altogether Indian." It was the largest grant ever made by the Crown to an individual.

After New Wales was rejected as a name for the colony, Penn suggested "Sylvania" to which the king added with "Penn" in honor of the admiral.

Because of the temperate government framed by Penn, which granted unprecedented freedoms and participation in the passage of laws, coupled with the excellent farmland, Pennsylvania soon began to attract a vast influx of settlers of diverse backgrounds—Quakers from England and Europe, Germans, Scotch-Irish and others. Inhabitants of the scattered Swedish villages were also brought into the colony as citizens.

In 1682, a year after the original settler arrived, Penn himself visited the colony and, sailing up the Delaware River, he reached the Swedish settlement of Wicaco. Here Penn decided was an excellent site for the provincial capital, which was to become Philadelphia.

Pennsylvania as a colony had its problems, including a long-running boundary dispute with Lord Baltimore—a dispute that wasn't resolved for some 80 years until a couple of surveyors named Mason and Dixon.

But in comparison with many other colonies, Pennsylvania's pre-Revolutionary history was essentially one of peaceful and rapid growth. For example, in four years Philadelphia's population surpassed that of New York City, which had been founded some 60 years earlier. Nor were the western reaches of the colony harassed by Indians as others were because of the friendship and trust established by Penn in the first days and seldom violated either individually or collectively by the Pennsylvanians.

On two separate occasions, the original charter governing the colony was revised, each time granting the residents even greater voice in the operation of the colony.

While his colony was prospering, Penn was experiencing major difficulties in his personal life. His running dispute with Lord Baltimore kept him in England, his wife and eldest son died, he was deprived of his colony by William and Mary on the suspicion he supported the deposed James II and he was incarcerated for two years on the charge. His proprietorship restored, Penn made his last trip to the colony in 1701. Upon his return, he discovered the last of his fortune had been looted by his thieving steward. He was stricken with paralysis and died in 1718 an invalid.

Which brings us to the last of the 13 original colonies—Georgia.

Founded in 1732, some 40 years after North Carolina was officially separated from South Carolina, it was the only colony to be set up directly by England's Parliament. It was named in honor of the reigning monarch, George II.

The colony as the brainchild of James Oglethorpe, a prominent member of the gentry and a member of Parliament, in the aftermath of what was the first market crash in the capitalistic world—the "South Sea Bubble." The South Sea Company was the largest enterprise of the day to sell public stock in a venture that promised the wealth of the South Seas to the investors.

There was a stampede of investors but, when foreign investors withdrew their money, a stampede in the reverse direction followed. "Panic set in, triggering off the company's ruin, and leaving hundreds of investors either with huge losses or bankrupt."[2] It also resulted in severe crowding in debtor's prison.

It occurred to Oglethorpe that a new colony would give these debtors a place to start over. It would also provide an addition haven for persecuted Protestants and, of interest to the Crown, it would provide a buffer between the Spanish in Florida and the royal colony of South Carolina.

Parliament granted a 21-year charter to a board of trustees in 1733 for land between the Savannah and Altamaha Rivers extended westward to the South Sea.

Perhaps because of the perceived spiritual needs of the original beneficiaries of Oglethorpe's philanthropy, the colony seemed to be a magnet for religious figures of the day, including John Wesley, the founder of Methodism, and the noted preacher George Whitfield.

As governor, Oglethorpe's military experience came in handy in dealing with incursions by the Spanish. He was less successful in enforcing the rather restrictive rules that were set out in the charter, including the prohibition on slavery and intoxicating liquor. Settlers also wanted a say in the operation of the colony, particularly as regards the land system, which granted each settler only a small farm, which had to pass down through the male side of the family.

After 18 years, the colony numbered about 1,000 widely scattered families and even at the time of the Revolution its capital Savannah was still a wooden village. In 1749, Parliament relaxed its restriction on the importation of slaves, but three years later the trustees gave up on the idea and surrendered their charter, and so Georgia became a royal colony.

"From the Northern seaboard to the Southern, the English had been able to maintain or to impose their basic institutions on all competing cultures."[3]

For about 100 years, the east coast of North America was essentially English, which in some ways made dealings between the colonials and London easier, since they shared a common background.

"During the 18th Century, however, the ethnic homogeneity was rudely and finally shattered as German, Swiss, Scotch-Irish, Africans and peoples of other stocks migrated or were imported in such substantial numbers that by the time of the Revolution half the population south of New England was non-English."⁴

Chapter 4

In the roughly 150 years between the founding of Jamestown and the Treaty of Paris, the 13 colonies had pieced together a varied tapestry of economic endeavors.

To a great extent, the economies in the various colonies were shaped by geography, topography and climate, but in the earliest stages they all faced common problems—food and shelter. Between the seemingly unbounded timber and the game it sheltered as well as the fish from the sea, the barest essentials were at hand everywhere the colonists looked.

But in those parlous times, there were yet two other necessities that were the opposite sides of the same coin—safety from potential enemies and communication with their friends. The answer in both cases was the same—the sea lanes.

In this instance, the early immigrants had ample guidance. The original instructions to the Virginia Company in 1606, for example, carefully spelled out where to settle—"you shall do your best endeavor to find out a safe port in the entrance to some navigable river, making choice of such a one as runneth farthest into the land"—and cautioned "be not hasty in landing your victuals and munitions" because "if you make many removes, besides the loss of time, you shall greatly spoil your victuals and your caske."[1]

Unfortunately, the founders of Jamestown followed the instructions without exercising some common sense, siting the colony in a very unhealthy environment, much to their detriment.

Locating far upriver beyond the reach of sea-going vessels was also a matter of protection. The company was also given directions on splitting the immediate chores—building a storehouse for the victuals, preparing the ground for planting, posting sentries for advance warning of an enemy and exploring the area around the settlement.

In the New England colonies, where the impetus for migration was primarily religious, settlers tended to come in groups—families or even full congregations. Boorstin describes the Massachusetts Bay Colony as "a community of self-selected conformists."[2] This thread of commonality encouraged them to gather in clusters that became the nucleus of townships. Large farms were uncommon because of the thin and generally rocky soil, leading to subsistence farming. Common grazing grounds and woodlots served the entire community.

Because of the large influx of immigrants in a relatively sort time—some 20,000 flowing into Massachusetts in a 15-year period between 1630 and 1645—the towns grew rapidly, fast enough that trade grew at more rapid pace than in most colonies. But the commonality extended only so far, even among Puritans. There were disagreements on matters of religious form and substance. "A dissension which in England would have created a new sect within Puritanism simply produced another colony in New England."[3]

The incoming immigrants brought a variety of essential skills with them. They also brought one other essential—cash. In many cases, the voluntary migrants liquidated their holdings in England in preparation for the trans-Atlantic voyage, meaning they had the wherewithal to purchase such necessities as were available when they arrived. The later the arrivals, the more the merchants on hand to greet them.

By 1630, Massachusetts stores sold all kinds of fabrics, some of which didn't meet with ecclesiastic approval. In the mid-1600s, the Massachusetts General Court felt constrained to pass laws against elaborate textiles and lace based on religious considerations. Not that textile production itself was taboo. Although textile production was theoretically in violation of British Navigation Act of 1651, in 1656, the Massachusetts General Court assessed each family for a quantity of cotton, wool or flax spun with a fine for each pound short.

Always a sea-faring nation, the English of New England almost naturally turned to the natural assets at hand. Large stands of pine and oak combined with a number of good harbors lent themselves to ship building, ship building led to fishing and eventually coastal trading. "The cod industry alone quickly furnished a basis for prosperity."[4] Boston soon became America's greatest port.

In the absence of overland routes connecting the widely separated dots that were the original settlements, ship building was a common industry all up and down the coast. In most cases, the ships were intended for either coastal trading or open ocean sailing to foreign ports.

"Building their own vessels and sailing them to ports all over the world, the shipmasters of Massachusetts Bay laid the foundation for a trade that was to grow steadily in importance. By the end of the colonial period, one-third of all vessels under the British flag were built in New England."[5]

But there were many designs developed for special purposes, such as the New England dory for open water fishing and the tobacco boat of Virginia particularly designed to float hogsheads from the plantation to the seaport. By the mid-1700s, southern colonies like South Carolina were rivaling New England in their production of seacraft.

Meanwhile, the colonies north of Maryland were commercial, dependent on trade in timber, molasses and slaves. The middle colonies attracted Dutch spinners and weavers despite prohibition against textile manufacture by Dutch West India Company, owners of New Netherlands, another display of mercantilism, this time of the Dutch variety.

The Dutch also left a legacy that slowed the growth of New York for generations. When New Amsterdam became New York in 1664, the English not only confirmed the huge land grants made to the patroons but surpassed them in new grants, some as much as 300,000 acres to land monopolists.[6] Since unimproved land was not taxed, the landowners were in no hurry to either develop or sell, except at their price.

As a result, land became scarce and expensive, encouraging settler to move on to the Jerseys or Pennsylvania, where 100 acres could be had for about £5. Over time, squatters moved into the large holdings, prompting land riots that, in some instances, required troops to quell.

Pennsylvania was the most cosmopolitan colony with English, Welsh, Irish, Dutch, German and Quaker settlers with textile manufacturing experience centered around Philadelphia and Germantown. Land grants were often given to professional weavers as inducement to migrate. Philadelphia grew the fastest of the five seaboard cities because of "the richness of the interior it served" in wheat, flour, bread, beef, pork, butter as well as lumber, iron and furs.[7] The city, according to traveler Peter Kalm in 1748, "came into being within one man's lifetime."[8]

Southern colonies were agricultural dependent on rice, tobacco, cotton, indigo, silk exports to England. Unlike the compact New England settlements that fostered a market for artisans, the large, spread out plantations of the South were forced to import their own, often indentured, help.[9] One attraction of indentured labor was that it was certain, at least for the period of the indenture. With land plentiful and cheap in some colonies, any skillful artisan could quit his employer and go into business for himself or take up farming.[10]

In some respects, the immigrants to the southern colonies, especially Virginia, had a more difficult time establishing flourishing settlements than did the New Englanders.

"Between 1607 and 1622, the Virginia Company transported some 10,000 people to the colony (Jamestown), but only 20 percent were still alive there in 1622."[11] The attrition was attributable to the poor site location that bred disease and the hostile reaction of native Indians to the treatment accorded them by the English, who attempted the same method of dealing with the incumbents as they had applied in Ireland.

By the early 1600s, the settlers around the Chesapeake were shipping glass, pitch, tar, potash and clapboards back to England[12], but these exports were not close to offsetting the expenses of the colony and it tottered on toward bankruptcy.

About 1618, the Virginia proprietors changed their policies, allowing free land to settlers and thus providing an incentive for productive labor. About the same time, the settlers finally hit on the product that was to prove their salvation—an import from the West Indies, tobacco.

"Virginia's tobacco production surged from 200,000 pounds in 1624 to three million pounds in 1638 as the Chesapeake outstripped the West Indies to become the principal supplier of tobacco to Europe."[13]

Profits to the proprietors were immense, with tobacco selling for five to 10 times its cost of production. Along with a measure of riches came an upswing in population, with the numbers in the Chesapeake area growing from 13,000 in 1650 to 41,000 twenty years later.

Virginia planters eventually became victims of their own success. Shipments exploded from three million pounds in 1638 to about 10 million pounds by the end of the 1660s and the planters were riding a runaway train. Because of the more than adequate supply, the price fell from two shillings a pound in 1620 to two pence a pound in the late 1650s. But it was to get worse.

"The swelling number of producers and their increased productivity glutted the English market, depressing the price of tobacco below the costs of production. With one penny a pound the minimum tobacco price for breaking even, planters faced ruin during the late 1660s and early 1670s, when the price plummeted to only half a penny a pound."[14]

As smaller planters failed, the larger plantations became larger and tobacco remained a mainstay of the Virginia and Maryland colonies for another century. In 1763, tobacco accounted for £768,000 out of a total export of £1.04 million.

With the lower price per pound, planters were forced to grow and export more and more to maintain their income. But since a given field could be planted only three years before becoming exhausted, tobacco required more and more land—and more and more labor—to maintain production figures.

The tobacco boom came too late to save the Virginia Company and it failed in 1624, James I revoked the charter and Virginia became a royal colony.

Eight years later, Charles I split off 12 million acres on the northern end of Chesapeake Bay and handed it to the Calvert family and it became Maryland.

"The largest concentration of population in 1750 lay in the two tobacco colonies, Virginia and Maryland, which together had more people—372,000—than any other region. Second to them were the four colonies of New England with 359,000 The four middle colonies numbered 294,000, Pennsylvania of course vastly overshadowing the others. New York, hampered by its vast patents and ungenerous land policies, grew slowly and ranked in 1750 as a small or medium-sized colony little larger in population than New Jersey. Most of the 142,000 people of the three colonies of the deeper South were divided, more or less evenly, between North and South Carolina. The small buffer state of Georgia, still struggling after 18 years to establish itself, had only about 5,000 colonists."[15]

The heavy reliance on very labor intensive crops also drove one of the other major colonial industries—slavery.

History says the first slaves were introduced into North America in 1619 by the Dutch when a ship landed with some 20, which were in due course sold. Not that slavery was a new phenomenon. From the dawn of recorded history, slavery has been the lot of conquered people as has been documented in ancient Central America, Egypt, Greece and Rome.

In fact, the incidence of slavery in North America was not really outstanding for the period.

"The North American colonies were only on the fringes of the immense South Atlantic system of slave trading and slave exploitation, which was mainly an affair of Central and South America and the sugar islands of the Caribbean." According to Hofstadter[16], only about five percent of the slaves came to the colonies.

But for the southern colonies, slavery became a necessity.

"At first, the southern colonies were able to rely on indentured servants (mostly, criminals, the poor, etc.) but as working conditions improved in the middle colonies and deteriorated in the south, they were unable to attract, or keep, enough indentured servants to supply the intensive labor required by tobacco, indigo, cane and rice. Additionally, the mortality rates in the swampy coastal regions of the Tidewater were extremely high. When it became known that many Africans were immune to the affects of malaria, they became the worker of choice for the planters."[17] "The high mortality rate among British migrants caused investors to turn their attention to African slaves."[18]

"Despite the importation of 15,000 indentured servants

between 1625 and 1640, Virginia's population increased by only 7,000."[19]

During the first half of the 17th Century Dutch New Amsterdam was "the chief North American slaving port . . ."[20] although the actual number of slave may have been rather small.

"In 1650, enslaved Africans numbered only 300, a mere two percent of the Chesapeake population."[21] On the other hand, English servants "composed at least three-quarters of the emigrants to the Chesapeake during the 17th Century."[22]

The situation changed considerably after 1664, when Dutch New Amsterdam became English New York and, thanks primarily to New Englanders, the so-called "Triangular Trade" came into being.

There were, in fact several triangular trade routes in operation back and forth across the Atlantic. For example, the colonials shipped products to Europe, where they were traded for produce not available in England, thence to England, where the produce was exchanged for manufactured goods needed in the colonies.

But the triangular trade that remains in history, lasted longer than most and has the most unsavory reputation was the triangular trade involving the importation of African slaves. But the colonials did not invent it.

In Europe, ships would load in England or France with guns, ammunition and manufactured goods, exchange them for slaves in Africa, transport their human cargo to the Caribbean islands or the North American colonies, where they were exchanged for sugar, tobacco or cotton and then back to their home ports.

"The vast majority of slaves brought to American shores came in British hulls."[23] In 1660, the English government chartered the "Company of Royal Adventurers Trading to Africa." It was reorganized in 1663 with the avowed purpose of slave trading, shutting out other English merchants from the trade.

The company collapsed in 1667, but five years later the "Royal African Company" emerged with a royal monopoly in the slave trade. Between 1680 and 1686, the company transported an average of 5,000 slaves a year in a total of some 249 voyages to Africa.

Under continuing pressure from English merchants, the government opened the slave trade to all and the average annual importation of slaves jumped fourfold to 20,000 a year. While the English were liberal with their use of the word "liberty," what they meant was "among other enterprises, the liberty to buy and sell slaves."[24]

"In the century and a half of the slave trade, from the 1650s to 1807, between three and four million Africans were transported out of their homelands to the New World in British ships."[25]

With the bars now down, colonials were not far behind in copying the process, although their starting point was liquid rather than solid. Rum was the means of exchange rather than the manufactured goods available in Europe, but it proved perhaps even more popular.

The going price for one prime male slave was about 100 gallons of rum.[26] The slaves were then transported to the sugar islands of the Caribbean and exchanged for molasses for the distilling of more rum, and so the cycle was repeated until well after the Revolution. "Between 1709 and 1807," according to state archives, "Rhode Island merchants sponsored at least 934 slaving voyages to the coast of Africa bringing some 106,000 Africans to the New World."

The endeavor was obviously profitable for both the Rhode Islanders but the mother country as well.

"Rhode Island rum-and-slaves traffic yielded £40,000 a year for remittances to England."[27]

"Although slave trading was less important for the economies of the Northern colonies than of England, they too took to it, and early in the (17th) century Yankee slavers operating chiefly out of Newport and Bristol in Rhode Island

and in much smaller volume out of Boston, Salem and Providence, with a sprinkling of vessels out of Portsmouth, New London and New York."[28]

Rhode Island, particularly Bristol, took to the trade with avengeance, perhaps because the colony had little other than the output of its distilleries to trade.

"Newport (R.I.), the leading slave port, had at midcentury (1750) perhaps as many as 170 vessels, or roughly half its merchant fleet, engaged in slaving."[29]

"Rhode Island's only real income was the slave trade."[30]

The overall impact on the racial makeup of the tobacco colonies of Virginia and Maryland can be seen in the population figures. "The Negro population in 1700 was about 28,000 or about 11 percent (but that number might be high); by 1770, about 459,00, or 21.8 percent."[31] Most of those were concentrated in Virginia and Maryland. : "In 1750 there were about 236,000 (slaves) in the colonies and the number had trebled since 1730."[32]

In keeping with their mercantilist practices, the English kept an eye on the competition, which in the early 1600s was primarily the Dutch, who were becoming the common carrier for the world.

Since the days of Richard II (1377-99), the English had tried to take steps to protect their shipping, but it wasn't until about 100 years later under the Tudors and Stuarts that really serious measures began to be passed.

While the earlier regulations were all intended to benefit the mother country at the expense of the colonies, they may be said to fall into two categories—those designed to control the distribution of goods and, later, those intended to regulate the production of goods. While the colonists were able to live with—or evade—these, it became increasingly impossible to countenance when the regulations were directed toward raising revenue.

Mercantilist regulation in the 13 colonies began in the 1620s (less than 20 years after Virginia founded and the same year as the Plymouth colony) when "steps were taken" to protect the struggling Virginia colony by barring the importation into Britain of Spanish or Dutch tobacco. Additional acts were passed in 1650s and 1660s.

Initially, the American colonies received rather preferential treatment. The Long Parliament in 1642 exempted New England exports and imports from all duties and a few years later all goods carried in English vessels to the southern colonies were added to the free list.

The first of what are now known as the Navigation Acts was passed in 1651 under Cromwell aimed at Dutch. Among other things, it forbade foreign built or owned ships from trading with the colonies and those that did legally had to have three-quarters of its crew from England or the English colonies. Certain "enumerated" goods had to be shipped to England and then transhipped to foreign ports; colonial imports had to come through English ports.

The act generally followed principles laid down by the Tudor and early Stuart regimes and its provisions were similar to those of a law passed in 1494 under Henry VII "prohibiting the Irish from exporting any industrial product, except with an English permit, and through an English port, after paying English fees."[33]

No goods grown or manufactured in Asia, Africa or America should be transported to England except in English vessels and the goods of any European country imported into England must be brought in English vessels or in vessels of the country producing them. Since the Dutch were not a major producing nation but rather the common carriers for those that were, this pretty well cut them out of any export of import trade with England. The Dutch forthwith declared war on England to get act repealed. It failed. The Dutch needn't have worried too much, since "it was nowhere strictly enforced, and in New England scarcely at all."[34]

A second act, adopted in 1660, carried the same provision about exports and imports traveling in British vessels, but it added colonial ships, putting them on the same footing as the British. This added impetus to the already ongoing shipbuilding industry, particularly in New England. By 1700 it was reported that the American merchant fleet numbered some 1,500 vessels plying their trade over half the world.

The bad news was that England began restricting the trade in specific commodities. Among the first so-called "enumerated goods" that might not be exported to any country but England were tobacco, sugar, cotton, wool and dyeing woods. On arrival in England, these goods would be subject heavy duties.

A further revision in 1666 were the Corn Laws, adopted in favor of the British farmer, that effectively shut out all colonial grain from export to England. This set off yet another cycle. Shut off from a large source of agricultural income, settlers, particularly those in New England and New York, gradually turned to manufacturing of various sorts. This triggered still more restrictions on manufactured goods.

As the colonial commercial structure began to grow, the nature of the Navigation Acts also began to change, going from the general to the specific, from the distribution of goods to their manufacture. It was both good news and bad for the colonials.

Not content with these restrictions, the acts were added to in 1672, imposing the same heavy duties on goods shipped from colony to colony. Again, an indication of the growing commerce in these goods, a growth seen as contrary to England's mercantilist designs.

New Yorkers proved proficient. By 1708, it is estimated that the colony was producing three-quarters of the woolen and linen goods used in the colony and fur hats that were exported both to England and the West Indies. The matter came to a head in 1732 with the so-called Hat Act, which not only barred exporting of hats to England, foreign countries or even to other colonies, it also limited the number of persons a hat maker may employ.

In 1733, Parliament passed the Sugar Act (or Molasses Act) that imposed a 6p tax per gallon on foreign molasses, which in effect doubled the cost. It was "less a tax than a prohibition, an attempt to give the sugar planters of the British West Indies a monopoly on the North American trade at the expense of molasses that could be purchased more cheaply in French islands."[35] Not that the act did much good, since it was widely avoided and not vigorously pursued.

As mentioned earlier, for some 20 years—from about 1720 to 1742—the colonies enjoyed a period of "salutary neglect" under Sir Robert Walpole, George I's chief minister. While some of the early trade regulations were adopted during Walpole's tenure, he made little effort to enforce them.

With Walpole no longer in office, the Earl of Halifax assumed the presidency of the Board of Trade and Plantations in 1748, an agency established in 1696 under William III. It took over the colonial supervision from the Privy Council supposedly to keep track of colonial trade among other things. Halifax was determined to take a more aggressive approach to regulating the colonial trade, armed with special Admiralty Courts set up for the trial of offenders.

These courts were a further offense to the colonials since they were seen as stacked against them. They were established in far away places and defendants were, in effect, forced to prove their innocence.

Hubert Hall, writing in American History Review, is quoted as crediting Halifax, as president of the Board of Trade and Plantations, and Sir Thomas Robinson, as the departmental secretary of state, as being practically responsible for the disasters that brought Pitt to office.[36]

For a time, the regulations bore fruit for Great Britain. In 1759, for example, New England sent to England goods valued at £38,000 but purchased goods valued at £600,000.[37] In 1766, Franklin informed Parliament, Pennsylvania's exports to Britain were £40,000 while its imports from Britain were £500,000. Naturally, the colonies could not sustain this sort of disadvantage since English merchants wanted payment in specie. Were it not for the widespread smuggling, it would have been totally impossible.

An amended Sugar Act was passed in 1764 under Pitt with the duty cut in half, but it contained provisions for more stringent enforcement. "Pitt had wanted to enforce the Sugar Act to stop American trade with the French." [38] It was, according to Reid "the first statute distinctly to tax the colonies rather than regulate trade."[39]

However, there had been previous voices raised in England advocating the North American colonies as a source of revenue through taxation.

"For it was precisely at this time that alarm was being caused by the schemes of the ministry and the suggestions of governors like (William) Shirley of Massachusetts, Bernard of New Jersey, and (Robert) Dinwiddie of Virginia (1751-58), for raising a war revenue on the colonies and overriding their chartered rights. In 1754, as later in 1756 and 1760, the 'British ministry heard one general clamor from men in office for taxation by act of Parliament.' "[40]

On the other hand, goods that were also produced in England—grain, salt provisions and fish—were not added to the enumerated list for a simple economic reason. If the colonial production could only be sent to England and that quantity was added to the domestic production, the island could not absorb it and prices would be driven down, to the detriment of domestic producers.

Colonial tobacco growers also enjoyed favored treatment, with heavy tariffs being placed on Spanish tobacco and a ban on tobacco growing in Ireland. A heavy tariff on Swedish iron also reflected to the colonials' benefit, at least for the time being. But by 1750, faced with the increase in colonial production, Parliament decreed in the Iron Act there were to be no rolling or slitting mills tolerated in the colonies, nor any furnace for making steel.

Although these measures directed against manufacturing were felt to a degree in the agricultural southern colonies since they made it more difficult to obtain a hat from New York or iron goods from New England, they were primarily felt in the northern and middle colonies.

Despite the variety of laws intended to regulate and direct trade in the colonies, they proved to be virtually impossible to enforce. There were too many miles of coastline to patrol, too many small settlements scattered over thousands of square miles to keep an eye on. Where officers were sent to the colonies as customs agents, they were drawn from the ill-trained ranks and susceptible to bribery.

Smuggling in many parts of the colonies was so common that it was raised to the level of respectability.

While New England traded illegally, the burden of the Navigation Acts fell more heavily on the southern colonies because a larger share of their products—e.g. rice and tobacco—went for export

There were some benefits to the colonies. Protection from foreign competition aided the New England ship builders, South Carolina received a subsidy on its indigo production, North Carolina received bounties on tar, pitch, turpentine and lumber. On balance, however, the restrictions benefited English merchants more than it benefited the colonists. Enforcement was lax.

Additional acts were passed in 1660, 1662, 1663, 1670, 1673 and 1696/1699. Each successive act further tightened the noose around the neck of colonial commerce. But there was one saving grace—enforcement, or rather the lack of it.

While it might not have been apparent to the English regarding the effect of their trade regulations on the North American colonies, others—particularly the French—seemed more discerning.

In 1730, (Charles Louis de Secondat, Baron de) Montesquieu had prophesied that "because of the laws of navigation and trade, England would be the first nation abandoned by her colonies."[41] About the same time, (Rene-Louis de Voyer de Paulmy, Marquis d') Argenson predicted the colonies would arise against the mother country. A similar prediction was made in 1750 by (Anne Robert Jacque) Turgot and was repeated in 1763 by (Charles Gravier, Comte de) Vergennes when the provisions of the Treaty of Paris were revealed.

But the British government was seemingly unwilling to take any advice, least of all from the French.

There were two other factors at work that distinguished life of the North American colonists from their brethren who remained at home—factors that mitigated against the formation of a nobility here. They were literacy and mobility.

While there was an appreciation for the classics among the English upper classes—Homer's Odyssey was translated into English by Alexander Pope in 1725—little attention was paid to educating the masses in England since the nobility saw no need for it. Better that the masses remain in their properly subservient place. Even into the 1700s, criminals could escape serious punishment by pleading the "right of clergy" by proving they could read from the Scriptures.

In the New England colonies in particular, literacy was a conscious objective so that the Puritan progeny could be properly instructed by reading the Bible. Many of the early immigrants brought their little libraries with them and English booksellers did a brisk business exporting their wares to the colonies.

Boston's Harvard College was founded in 1636 and three years later the first printing press in the English colonies was installed within its walls. The General Assembly in 1647 enacted the "ye olde deluder Satan" act requiring every town of 50 families to set up a grammar school, which obviously created the need the teachers to staff them.

A few years later the Collegiate School of Connecticut—later to become Yale University—was established in New Haven. Quakers also set store in education and the first

Pennsylvania school was established in 1683 that taught, among other things, the keeping of accounts.

As Philadelphia grew, so did the number of its educational institutions, many offering free education to those unable to pay. While night schools might be considered a new idea, they existed in Philadelphia in the 1700s. Much of what happened educationally in Philadelphia is attributable to Benjamin Franklin, who, it will be remembered, came to the city as a printer's devil. The public academy he took an active part in founding in 1740 was the nucleus of what was to become the University of Pennsylvania.

Virginia, while taking a generally dim view of public education, was home to William and Mary College near the end of the century, but in general education in the colony took a rather different path. Because of the lack of centers of population, plantation owners were more apt to import tutors—often from Ireland or Scotland—to teach their children. The more wealthy sent their children to England for their studies.

A literate population was not content just to read the Scriptures. Boston and Philadelphia bookstalls found a ready market for the classics and philosophy. It was said that the second most popular printed import after the Bible was Blackstone's law books, which might have sent a signal to the aristocracy if they had been looking or listening.

By 1704, the ability to read became so widespread and the population so curious about the world around them that the first newspaper was printed in Boston. In 1729, Benjamin and James Franklin began publishing "The Pennsylvania Gazette" and by 1745, there were 22 newspapers being published throughout the colonies.

Two legal actions—one in New York and the other in London almost exactly 30 years apart—serve to cast a spotlight on the differences between attitudes exhibited toward journalism on opposite sides of the Atlantic.

In 1732, Peter Zenger, publisher of the New York Weekly

Journal, was decidedly anti-government and the governor had him jailed on a charge of seditious libel. Zenger managed to continue his publication throughout the nine months of his trial. Andrew Hamilton, Zenger's defense attorney, argued that the charges printed by Zenger were in fact true and therefore not libelous. The jury agreed and one of the basic tenets of freedom of the press was created.

The fate of London publisher and member of Parliament John Wilkes in 1763 was far different. Wilkes, in his North Briton, made allusions to the common supposition there was more between Lord Bute and George III's mother than was proper and also implied that the king had lied in a speech. Wilkes was thrown into the Tower of London. The general warrant also covered "the authors, printers and publishers of the North Briton, No. 45."[42] A sympathetic crowd prevented the seized edition from being burned. A London jury even found for monetary compensation to Wilkes' printers.

Wilkes was eventually released from the Tower and expelled from Parliament. Twice more he was re-elected and twice more expelled. He eventually became Lord Mayor of London. While the will of the people finally prevailed, it was over the objections of both the king and nobility. No point of law was settled and the antagonism between the nobility and the masses was continued.

If literacy prevented the North American colonists from being kept in ignorance, mobility kept them from being kept chained by economics.

In England, surrounded on all sides by water, the physical room for maneuver—disregarding for the moment the societal problems involved in moving from place to place—was limited. England and Wales cover about the same area as present day Florida and, with Scotland thrown in it equals little more than Utah or Minnesota. Even though the population was less than six million—and nearly a tenth of that concentrated in London—it was still rather close quarters.

Small wonder that the young and able-bodied were willing to gamble a six—or seven-year indenture to cover the £6 fare to America and a chance for what they expected to be a better life.

Of course, the land within the colonial boundaries was not limitless. Eventually, the eastern seaboard—especially in New England—became saturated and western migration became a necessity.

This westward thrust was technically halted by the Peace of Paris that ended the Seven Years War in 1763 when the fall line of the Appalachian Mountains was established as a western limit to migration.

Which proved once again to be seen by the colonials as another irritant to be addressed forcefully in just a few years.

Chapter 5

Having looked at some of the commercial and religious aspects of England's growth into the middle 1700s, we come to the Seven Years War, the conflict that made her the preeminent power in Europe and brought politics to the forefront.

No historical incident is complete unto itself, but springs from the past and projects into the future. Roots of the French and Indian War, as the English colonists in North America were to call the struggle, went back a long way. It was the fourth in a series of major wars between England and France, a series that began in 1689.[1] (There was one more to come; the quelling of a Corsican named Bonaparte.)

The preceding three clashes had been predominantly European affairs, but the American colonies had not been insulated from their effects. On each previous occasion two or more colonies were involved as suppliers of provisions or troops.[2] These conflicts were separated by varying periods of uneasy peace, at least on paper, but so continuous was the fighting that it was hard to distinguish official from unofficial wars.

The continuity of ill feeling between England and France, stemming from religious, political and economic sources, is well-illustrated by the Seven Years War.

According to formalities, war was declared in 1756, ending a supposed eight-year peace that came after they and Austria had stopped fighting over who would occupy the Austrian throne. However, the Treaty of Aix-la-Chapelle (1748) ending the War of the Austrian Succession settled nothing outside continental Europe since "every man of colonial origin, English and French alike, saw that the treaty . . . was merely an armistice."[3]

Treaty or no treaty, the leading edges of the French and English colonial empires continued to rub each other the wrong way wherever they touched. In India, there was barely a brief truce.[4] There, the competition was between the English East India Company, established in 1600, and the French Compagne des Indies Orientales (founded in 1664). When England and France opposed each other in the War of the Austrian Succession "technically the two companies were placed in a state of war."[5]

Neither company hesitated to take advantage of the technicality and, with sundry East Indian allies, waged the First Carnatic War to an inconclusive halt.

A year's respite followed the Peace of Aix-la-Chapelle before the Second Carnatic War flared. With Great Britain's control of the seas, it was only a matter of time for the French. Even so, the fighting dragged on seven years before Marquis Joseph Francois Dupleix, governor-general of French India and "one of France's greatest empire builders"[6] sued for peace with Robert Clive, who had risen from a clerkship in the East India Company to commander of its forces. A three-month truce was arranged pending approval of the formal treaty by their home governments. But the treaty was never ratified thanks to the outbreak of the Seven Years War.[7]

In North America, the years leading up to the French and Indian War were no more tranquil. After a century of exploration, the French by the late 1740s had established a line of outposts down the St. Lawrence River, through the Great Lakes and the Ohio River country and down the Mississippi to its mouth.

No sooner was the ink dry of the Treaty of Aix-la-Chapelle then they started pushing even further south and east into the Ohio Valley. Their intent was "to confine the English colonists to the area between the Atlantic and the Alleghanies . . ."[8] At the same time, English colonists, particularly those Virginians forming the Ohio Company, were moving westward over the mountains to exploit the same ground.

This company, which included among its founders George Washington's brothers Lawrence and Augustine, was set up in Virginia in 1747 and two years later was granted 200,000 acres by that state from its western claims.[9] Skirmishes were sharp and frequent with settlements destroyed, prisoners taken and mutual eviction notices served.[10]

Which, if indeed any, of these individual actions actually triggered the French and Indian War is hard to say. One author pinpoints Washington's expedition of 1754 into the Ohio country when, at the head of a small band, he surprised a French ensign, Coulon de Jumonville, "who was carrying to the English an order to evacuate the valley of the Ohio, which both nations claimed. Jumonville and some of his party were killed. This was the first blood of the conflict."[11] This "order" might be considered somewhat imprudent of the French since in the 1750s "the British colonists outnumbered the colonists of New France by 23 to 1."[12]

More dramatic is another author's reconstruction of the Washington-Jumonville encounter. "'Fire' was the clear command that rang out through the forest, and the first volley of a great war went flying on its mission of death."[13]

On the other hand, Beard[14] dates the war's beginning with Gen. Edward Braddock's expedition at the head of two

British regiments in 1755 into the western lands claimed by Pennsylvania "where they suffered a disastrous defeat" at the hands of the French and their Indian allies along the shores of the Monongahela River.

Initial reaction by the Provincials to French expansion was piecemeal and haphazard. Some organized efforts to dispute the area were made by Massachusetts, the Ohio Company and Virginia (which had commissioned Washington's forces that met Jumonville). Most of the fights, however, were strictly personal on the part of the colonials involved.

The Albany Congress, as it is called, was convened at the behest of the English Board of Trade and the Privy Council so that the colonies from Virginia northward might bolster their ties with their Indian allies in the Six Nations,. construct a string of forts along their western border and cooperate in the supply of men and materials to man them.

New York Lieutenant Governor James De Lancey invited eight colonies to send delegates. New Jersey, which had neither a western boundary or any claims to western lands, and Virginia, which had already been promised aid from London, declined.

Not that the colonials were unmindful of the value of concerted action. "Every Body cries, a Union is absolutely necessary"[15] but they were unable to make up their minds on what kind.

Eventually, 25 delegates from the other six colonies gathered at Albany for one more attempt at developing a trans-colony plan of mutual assistance. Over the preceding 50 years, numerous attempts to achieve the same goal had proven fruitless as each colony was more jealously concerned with its individual needs than with common defense.

Beard states that one of the purposes of the Albany Congress was to bring the colonies together under "articles of union and confederation with each other for mutual defense of his majesty's subjects in time of peace as well as war."[16] But there was more.

London was of the belief that the combined colonies could present a united front against the encroachments of the French to the west, a view supported by Massachusetts Governor William Shirley. Both London and Shirley were also concerned that the colonies were growing in 13 different directions and increasingly less under control of the British government. A single, unified colonial structure suitably subservient to London, they reasoned, would be easier to control than 13 separate governments.

Shirley sent Thomas Hutchinson as the colony's representative to the Albany gathering, but Hutchinson had his own reasons for supporting mutual assistance. His objective was "the utter destruction of New France."[17]

One after the other, various plans—notably those of Pennsylvania and New York—were rejected and a committee appointed to try to come up with a comprehensive proposal.

What evolved strongly resembled a plan that had been jotted down by Benjamin Franklin en route to the conference. Discussions of the idea during this first Continental gathering brought to the surface streams of political thought from both sides of the Atlantic, streams that were to become diverging torrents in the years ahead.

Failure of Franklin's Albany Plan of Union, only a week after Washington was forced to surrender Fort Necessity to the French and withdraw east of the Alleghanies, was a measure of that divergence.

"The assemblies . . . thought there was too much prerogative in it" Franklin wrote, "and in England it was judged to have too much of the democratic."[18]

Rejection by the assemblies, therefore, "spared the English government the embarassment of having to veto it."[19]

While the Provincials talked abut federation; while poorly equipped French troops sought dominance in the Ohio Valley, and while the English colonies resisted in random fashion, affairs were not much better on the Continent, where a lady harbored great ill will against Frederick the Great.

In 1740, Frederick and his Prussian army had taken the province of Silesia from Austria, much to the displeasure of Empress Marie Theresa "who never reconciled herself to the loss."[20] But since Prussia was allied with France (for 200 years a bitter enemy of Austria) and since England (her supporter in the late War of the Austrian Succession) was not in the market for another war at the moment, there was little she could do. The came the Diplomatic Revolution, a realignment of alliances so dramatic that it belongs to "the seven wonders of diplomatic history."[21]

As the year 1755 moved into autumn, Frederick began to have doubts about France. He felt Louis XV would try to avoid his commitments if it came to war. Of even more importance, Russia had signed a new defense pact with England to protect George's Hanoverian possessions. Diplomatic relations between the two countries went back a decade and there was always a possibility of England, Russia and Austria ganging up on him. ":The time had not yet come when Frederick could face the idea of having Prussia carry on a war against three great powers with only one single slippery ally like France."[22]

In London, George II, ruler of Great Britain and uncle to Frederick, had been fretting since the start of the War of Austrian Succession that his nephew might take it into his head to expropriate George's hereditary electorate of Hanover, "a possession dearer to his heart than the kingdom of Great Britain."[23] Additionally, relations with France in North America were worsening.

Thus, when nephew demonstrated a willingness to become an ally, uncle was willing to listen. The result was the Convention of Westminster signed in 1756 pledging mutual peace, friendship and defense. The convention also annulled the subsidy treaty concluded between England and Russia the year before.[24]

Berlin and London were not the only capitals where delicate negotiations were underway. Vienna and Versailles were also considering a few changes. Maria Theresa had long since come to the conclusion that Austria's security was more threatened by Prussia than France. Besides, Frederick was a heretic[25] The Viennese ambassador turned his full attention toward undermining the Versailles-Berlin axis. It almost turned into a race to see who could engineer the shift first. Frederick and his uncle won in January, 1756.

Faced with the Westminster Convention, Louis and Maria came to terms in May with the First Treaty of Versailles. Neither got all they wanted from the other. In return for a portion of the Austrian-held Netherlands, France agreed to help Austria is she were attacked. France would have liked all the Netherlands and Austria would have preferred an offensive treaty against Prussia,[26] but France was not to agree to this for another year.

Russia's Czarina Elizabeth, hating Frederick and being piqued with the English for voiding their 1755 treaty, was more than receptive to the Austrian emissaries. She and Maria concluded an offensive treaty at the outset. Sweden and Saxony joined against England and Prussia and, although still undeclared, the war flared in earnest.

Chapter 6

Both France and England opened the war under less than auspicious circumstances. England recovered from her fumbling ways while France did not, and the conflict soon devolved into a dreary succession of defeats for the colonial French armies, unsupported as they were by their home government.

With the Marquise de Pompadour, mistress of Louis XV, squandering millions on her "frivolous favorites" in Paris, French armies overseas went without supplies or reinforcements. "What else could come but disaster?" asks Watson.[1] Adds Fuller, "the royal government at Versailles depended on a corrupt and ill-paid bureaucracy to manage its colonial affairs."[2]

England, her land forces reduced to 18,000 men[3], delegated the waging of a land war in Europe to Frederick and his Prussians and proceeded to employ her two-to-one superiority over the French at sea to telling advantage. About a month after the signing of the First Treaty of Versailles, the English seized French ships of the line *Alcide* and *Lys*, part of the French fleet bound for the New World with reinforcements for garrisons there. This was followed by "a general seizure of French merchant ships . . ."[4] as many as 300 carrying cargo valued at 30,000,000 livres and the impressment of their 10,000 crewman[5]

Land wars in Europe and India had only indirect effects in North America. Demolition of French influence in India had a definite impact on English economy and contributed greatly to the erection of the first British empire, while Frederick's fast and furious marching and countermarching played a large role in shaping future European history.

But those events of greatest concern to those interested in American history took place in England's council chambers, on the waters of the Mediterranean and Atlantic and in the wooded reaches of the New World.

At the onset of the Seven Years War, neither France nor England were overendowed with high-caliber leaders in positions of power. Under Louis XV's "vicious" system of government, only the select few ruled "and among those select few no statesman appeared."[6] England was so unfortunate as to have as prime minister a man "who could not command the respect of his own servants"[7] and who had been termed by his majesty George II as "the impertinent fool"[8]—Thomas Pelham-Holles, the Duke of Newcastle, "the major Whig aristocratic grandee" and "a great political fixer."[9]

Despite an auspicious beginning, attested to by those French merchantmen lying in British harbors, it soon became clear that foolishness can be a greater handicap that viciousness.

Two military engagements, each relatively minor in itself, combined to change the composition of the British government and lift it to the highest level it was to reach in the Eighteenth Century. The first was the ill-fated expedition into the Pennsylvania hinterlands in 1755 led by Gen. Edward Braddock and the second was the loss the following year of the island of Minorca. One of the Balearic Islands in the western Mediterranean, its fine harbor at Mahon had been a British base for almost half a century.

Recognizing its strategic importance, the French dispatched a fleet under Roland Michel Barron, Comte de la Galissoniere, accompanied by 15,000 troops commanded by the Duke of Richelieu against a Minorca garrison "that had not been reinforced, and numbered a scant 3,000 men."[10] The British sent a fleet under Admiral John Byng to relieve the besieged port. The adequacy of the effort is open to question. Churchill called it "ill-equipped"[11] while Mahan credits the British with a 13-to-12 advantage in ships of the line.[12] The French did, however, have the advantage in troops with 15,000 against 3,000 English in the port and 4,000 with Byng.

In retrospect, Byng's plan of attack against the blockading French was not too well conceived nor pressed with the greatest vigor. LaGalissoniere, on the other hand, was perhaps more concerned with covering the forces on land than with destroying the British fleet.[13] Byng's contingent was beaten off and "the English soothed their chagrin by shooting Byng"[14] in what Churchill calls "one of the most scandalous evasions of responsibility that an English government has ever perpetrated . . ."[15]

The Braddock fiasco raised some eyebrows in London, but the loss of Minorca and the ensuing court martial "raised a national outcry."[16]

Remarkably, the Minorca capture had little effect in France. A French naval officer, writing shortly afterward, states: "Incredible as it may seem, the minister of marine, after the glorious affair of Mahon, instead of yielding to the zeal of an enlightened patriotism and profiting by the impulse which this victory gave to France to build up the navy, saw fit to sell the ships and rigging which we still had in our ports."[17]

It took some time before the result of this shortsightedness made itself felt in France, but in England the incident placed the Newcastle government in disgrace and led to its dissolution.

The most important result of the outcry was an irresistible popular demand for the return of William Pitt to the inner councils of government. For nine years he had been Paymaster of the Forces, a post others had for years used to line their pockets. Pitt's refusal to do the same earned him the admiration of many and the nickname "The Great Commoner."

Pitt lost his post in November, 1755, when the king removed him after Pitt had scathingly attacked Newcastle in a speech before Commons. His was a leading voice from the opposition bench until the following June when George II, finally heeding the clamor, summoned him to form a new ministry. As Dr. Johnson described the situation: "Walpole was a minister given by the Crown to the people. Pitt was a minister given by the people to the Crown."[18] His first ministry was formed without Newcastle, but before many months Pitt was forced to the realization that he needed Newcastle's political power to implement his program. This brought about a realignment in 1757 with the agreement and understanding that Newcastle was to handle the patronage while Pitt concentrated on the war.[19]

"Tall, spare, hawk-nosed William Pitt, master orator and brilliant statesman"[20] was confident of his ability to win. "I know that I can save this country and that no one else can," he told the Duke of Devonshire, nominal head of the first Pitt ministry.[21] While it might be questionable whether there was no other man in the empire who could have done it, time proved Pitt correct in believing that he could. As "an unpleasant man, ruthless, arrogant and inconsistent"[22] he left a trail of bruised sensibilities behind him, a situation that was to react against him later.

To appreciate the magnitude of Pitt's accomplishments, it is necessary to picture the military situation at the beginning of his government. Arrayed against Great Britain and her sole ally, Prussia, were France, Austria, Russia, Sweden and Saxony. Frederick the Great had been pushed back into his own territory and was nearly encircled. British troops under the Duke of Cumberland, sent to defend George's Hanover and Brunswick possessions, had been defeated and had surrendered. The important naval base of Minorca was gone. In India, the French were putting up a strong defense and in Canada Montcalm was pushing southward against the American frontier.

Pitt may have had his failings, but wasting time was not one of them. Installed as Secretary of State, he gave full vent to his energies and rewrote the powers of that office to suit himself. He renounced Cumberland's surrender. With Louis XV's invasion threat of 1756 a thing of the past, foreign troops imported in that year to protect England were returned to the field on the Continent. Bills providing £670,000 subsidy for Frederick's campaigns were pushed through Parliament.[23]

Within the military, he cashiered admirals and generals to make room for younger men he felt more competent. He infused the military and the civilian population with confidence in place of depression and languor. The effect of his "aggressive, dominating personality" reached "even the youngest officer of the line, who felt that with Pitt in command failure might be forgiven but hesitation never."[24]

In formulating strategy for what Lawrence Gipson called "the Great War for the Empire," Pitt was pragmatist enough to retreat from previous positions taken as a member of the opposition.

Fifteen years earlier, during the War of the Austrian Succession, he had taken the government to task for engaging in a land war in Europe rather than conducting a naval and colonial war.[25] Now he decided that France (always considered the principal foe) had to be thoroughly defeated, not only overseas and on the seas but also on the Continent itself, or she would rise again.[26]

Some historians see it otherwise. "Pitt . . . saw that the quarrel between England and France was not to be decided in Europe and determined once and for all to crush the French in America."²⁷

From his Cleveland Row office, Pitt surveyed the worldwide scope of operations and drew his plans. It may be argued whether everything went according to his master plan, but with the drive emanating from London, things undeniably began to happen.

The same month he returned to government—June, 1757—Sir Robert Clive gained a smashing victory at Plassey that brought the province of Bengal under the British and "gave to the East India Company the control of northeastern India"²⁸ Military events from that point until the Battle of Pondicherry in January 1761 formed an almost uniform succession of British victories. With sound leadership of the land forces and control of the seas to prevent reinforcements from France, total British triumph on the subcontinent was inevitable.

The sea lanes to India were not the only stretches of water under British dominance. Operating out of Portugese ports, the British fleet clamped a tight surveillance on France's Atlantic harbors. This watch was later extended to the Mediterranean coast as well, effectively shutting off resupply to Canada as well as to India. Revival of French plans to invade England brought about the only major, concerted effort to break the blockade.

But when the Toulon fleet under de la Clue tried to concentrate at Brest in 1759, it was discovered by Boscawen's fleet and defeated in a "running fight ending in Lagos Bay in August." In fact, "Hawke and Boscawen's watch on the French Atlantic and Mediterranean ports had been so close that few ships of the line had been able to leave them during the year and French colonial possessions had become completely isolated."²⁹

After reorganizing the military services, providing finances for his Prussian ally, strengthening the British position in India and setting a sea watch on France, Pitt turned his attention to the far side of the Atlantic. The British commander-in-chief was John Campbell, Fourth Earl of Loudon (or Loudoun), "a rough Scottish lord, hot and irascible,"[30] but "an ineffectual and unenterprising officer."[31] Early in 1758 Pitt recalled Loudon "for whom he had a fierce contempt"[32] after the commander had accumulated British and colonial troops at Halifax for an assault in the fortress of Louisburg, an assault that never took place. Absence of the troops, however, provided the French and their Indian allies an opportunity to raid throughout the Hudson River valley, capture Fort William Henry and massacre part of its garrison.

In Loudon's place, Pitt sent Lord Jeffrey Amherst, newly promoted from lieutenant colonel to major general, to carry out a well-conceived three-pronged campaign, but one perhaps slightly too elaborate to be directed from 3,000 miles away.

The 1758 campaign called for Amherst, with Brigadier James Wolfe, a 30-year-old "prig and martinet,"[33] and naval support to take Louisburg and then drive up the St. Lawrence River to Quebec. The second prong, headed by General James Abercromby (or Abercrombie), was to seize Lake George and join Amherst and Wolfe at Quebec. Finally, Brigadier John Forbes was to lead a force up the Ohio Valley from Pennsylvania and take Fort Duquesne.[34]

Two of the three prongs met with some measure of success. Amherst's forces took Louisburg in July. Removal of that threat to New England soothed some of the sting of its restoration to France following the War of the Austrian Succession, an act that had struck New England "as the sorest affront which it had ever received at the hands of the home government."[34] Abercromby, in moving toward Lake George, ran into strong French emplacements at Fort Ticonderoga and was repulsed.

His operation was saved from total frustration, however, by virtue of the fact that before reaching Fort Ticonderoga he had reluctantly detached Lieutenant Colonel John

Bradstreet and 3,000 men (nearly all provincials) to penetrate the Mohawk Valley. Within a month after the fall of Louisburg, they overran Fort Frontenac with its store of provisions, munitions and boats. "Next to Louisburg, this was the heaviest blow that the French had yet received."[35]

Both ends of the St. Lawrence were now sealed and Forbes' mission was made easier. Forging his way out of the Pennsylvania wilderness and over the Alleghanies, he closed in on Fort Duquesne in the second half of November. With the loss of Fort Frontenac on Lake Ontario, the French felt their position untenable and withdrew from the fortifications. The British razed the defenses and memorialized their London leader by renaming the spot Fort Pitt, later altered to Pittsburgh.

The fall of Fort Duquesne marked the end of the campaigning for 1758 and the troops on both sides went into winter quarters. It was a hard winter for the Canadians and the French soldiers, thanks to a crop failure the preceding fall, a situation that led Montcalm to counsel his home government to accept peace "no matter what the boundaries."[36]

Although the troops were not in the field, the winter and spring were not wasted. Amherst was elevated to the post of commander-in-chief of the British forces in North America replacing Abercromby. Parliament, encouraged by the events of 1758, voted £12,000,000 sterling to continue the war and Pitt laid plans for 1759.

Once again, his strategy was based on a three-pronged offensive. General Prideaux was to take Fort Niagara and descend the St. Lawrence to Montreal. Amherst was to take the largest force and proceed against Fort Ticonderoga and Crown Point. Finally, Wolfe was to advance up the St. Lawrence and take Quebec.[38]

Fort Niagara fell July 25, breaking communications between Canada and Louisiana. Amherst met with equal success, moving through the Lake Champlain country in the same month and taking both objectives without a major battle with the retreating French.[37] Wolfe and his force arrived before Quebec late in June, where the defenders were commanded by General Louis Joseph de Montcalm, setting the stage for the most famous face-to-face encounter in pre-Revolutionary history.

After a month on the river bank, all the British had to show for their efforts was the reduction of the lower part of the city by their artillery and the loss of about 500 troops in a frontal assault on the city. August passed in indecision and thoughts of winter added to the urgency of the situation. For the British ships to be trapped by ice in the river would be unqualified disaster.

Finally, in September, the British slipped downriver past the city at night, landed and threaded their way up a narrow trail to the top of the steep bluffs. Brushing aside a small French outpost, the troops formed on the Plains of Abraham in the nearly undefended rear of the city as dawn broke.

The ensuing battle claimed the lives of both commanders and broke the French defenders. Five days later, Quebec was surrendered and 1759 ended with "the complete triumph of English arms."[38] The year 1760 saw a bid by the French to regain Quebec, a bid that ended with the spring thaw that brought British men of war back down the St. Lawrence. In September, Montreal fell to the British and, to all intents and purposes, the French and Indian War was over.

For France "on land the war was not fortunate; on the sea it was destructive."[39]

Six weeks after the fall of Montreal an event occurred to London that was to have a profound effect on the course of history, not only in England but also in the New World—George II was seized "with an apoplectic fit . . . and died in half an hour."[40] The 77-year-old monarch was succeeded by his 22-year-old grandson, George William Frederick—George III.

Chapter 7

George III was born (according to the modern calendar) June 4, 1738, at a time when relations between his father, Frederick, Prince of Wales, and his grandfather, George II, were at their worst. "It has often been supposed," says White, "that there was something pathological about the way that Hanoverian kings regularly quarreled with the eldest sons."[1] Pathological might not be a strong enough word to describe the situation.

Frederick's removal of his wife Augusta from Hampton Court at St. James Palace in July, 1737 with the birth of their first child imminent brought an open breach in the family. Not that the family relationship was good before that. As Prince of Wales, George II had received an annual income of £100,000. On his son, however, he settled only £38,000-£24,000 as Prince of Wales and £14,000 as Duke of Cornwall. On the occasion of his marriage in 1736 to Augusta, Frederick persuaded his friends in Parliament to introduce a resolution calling for the full £100,000. The resolution was defeated 234 to 204.[2]

Contemporary evaluations of "Poor Fred" ranged from active loathing to approbation. The king and queen made no secret of their feelings. Queen Caroline expressed the wish that the ground under her son's feet "would open this moment and sink the monster into the lowest hole in hell" while His Highness, if forced into his son's presence, passed him in stony silence.

The mad dash with the pregnant Augusta resulted in the couple and their new-born daughter (the first of nine children) being ordered from the king's palace "as soon as ever the safety and convenience of the Princess will permit."[3] Not content with that, His Majesty made public announcement "that whoever continued to pay court to the Prince and Princess would not be received by the King and Queen."[4]

But Fitzfrederick as his mother called him, was not without friends. Lord Egmont noted in his diary that many of those who witnessed the family leaving St. James Palace were in tears. Ironically, Frederick's popularity had somewhat the same base that so ill-pleased his son in later years when it manifested itself in William Pitt—the common people.

Neither George II nor Caroline his queen were overly congenial with the people. The street humor of December, 1736, when George was due back from one of his frequent trips to Hanover, included the question "How is the wind today for the King?" and the answer "Like the people, against him."[5] Egmont further notes that the queen was hissed at the opera "upon which others clapped."

Other contemporary judgments of Frederick from those in government included Robert Walpole's chain of adjectives that began with "poor, weak, irresolute" and extended through "dishonest, contemptible"; Henry Fox characterized him as "worthless." But he was governor of the Sadler's Company and, at least once, the crowd attending a play stood and cheered him.

Even today, judgments still vary. One source refers to him as "absurd"[6] while another grudgingly admits that "he seems to have been an affectionate husband and father."[7]

It would appear to be a fair reading to say that a split was appearing in the country and that Frederick was gaining more popularity than the royal couple felt comfortable with. "My God," the queen was quoted, "popularity always makes me sick; but Fitz' popularity makes me vomit."

Nor was Frederick without political power. As the Prince of Wales, Duke of Cornwall and a member of Parliament, he had certain patronage available to dispense. His group was active in the effort that resulted in Walpole's resignation in 1742. "It was the zenith of the Prince's career as a politician."[8]

Frederick did not lack in the social and intellectual graces either. He played the cello; his tree collection later blossomed into the Royal Botanical Gardens; he had a taste for art and his court included such poets as Pope and Swift. "Perhaps," says a latter-day author, "King George III's intellectual curiosity was first roused by his father."[9]

The resignation of Walpole, the granting of the prince's full allowance and vigorous prosecution of the War of the Austrian Succession by the Pelham-Newcastle administration temporarily deprived the prince and his followers of issues. But with the war ended, Pelham became concerned over "the increasing strength of the Prince's opposition."

Then, suddenly, in March, 1751, the prince caught a cold that eventually progressed into pleuresy. At mid-month, Bubb Doddington reported that the prince had apparently recovered, but five days later Fitzfrederick was seized with an uncontrollable "fit of coughing and spitting." Augusta was sent for, but her husband was dead when she reached his side.

In keeping with his character, even the cause of his death has been subject to question. An autopsy was held and death was attributed to a ruptured abscess in his chest. A second abscess was also discovered "supposed to have been of long standing and imputed to a blow"—understood to have been inflicted by a cricket ball during a game at Cliveden, the prince's Buckinghamshire country home, some three years previous.[10] The presence of the second abscess have led some current authors to attribute death to the delayed effects of the cricket, or tennis, ball.[11]

The widow, Princess Augusta, was 32 with nine children—one the heir apparent—to care for. Evaluations of the princes are nearly as mixed as those of her husband.

Married at 17 after being selected by George II and accepted by Frederick as the least disagreeable of several possibilities, she could speak no English and little French on her arrival in 1736.[12] Her new husband had been associating with the vocal opposition—including their "brightest star" William Pitt—for more than three years.

A year later, she and her husband and child are expelled from the royal court and sanctions pronounced against their friends. Even before that, the spiteful mouthings of her mother-in-law and the incivility of her father-in-law could hardly have escaped her notice, even if she couldn't understand the language—or perhaps Queen Caroline translated her remarks into German also.

For nearly half her married life, Augusta was either getting over a childbirth or preparing for the next. She undoubtedly presided over the prince's social gatherings and met his political allies, but little is found to indicate her sympathies or participation. A recent authority described her as a "foolish, ignorant woman."[13] It is unlikely that she was.

When Fitzfrederick died, his son George was 13. His father the king was 68, an advanced age for the times. This disparity in age brought up a natural question: Should the king die before his grandson reached majority, who would reign as regent?

A month after Frederick's death, George II recommended and Parliament agreed to name Princess Augusta as regent. Neither the king nor Parliament were under any compulsion to do so. She, in fact, is reported to have been deathly afraid the king would designate his second son, the Duke of Cumberland, as regent.

But the King was sufficiently aware of the widespread fear in which his second son was held, a fear springing from atrocities committed by his army in Scotland. The king decided that although Augusta was not particularly well liked, she was preferable to the feared Cumberland.

Remembering that George II's age made regency a distinct possibility, it is doubtful whether she would have been recommended or accepted if she had been either "foolish" or "ignorant."

Perhaps she was gullible. Claims one author, "Had her husband told her that the earth was flat or the moon made out of cheese, she would have believed him."[14] But on the other hand, Horace Walpole pictured her as a "passionate and domineering woman" conspiring with her lover, Lord Bute, to steer her inexperienced son into actions "designed to increase the prerogative of the Crown."

It is probably safe to assume that she was something in between these extremes. She was judged worthy enough to be named regent (albeit with an appointed advisory council to assist her). As something of a quid pro quo for the regency, which soothed her fears of Cumberland, she did not object too strenuously to the appointed overseers of her sons' education. She remained, however, "suspicious, prim, conscientious, censorious."[15]

She had sense enough to maintain at least a civil relationship with the king. She had gumption enough to resist the king's wish to remove the two eldest boys from her presence at an early age.

Until the young Prince George became heir apparent, there was little remarkable in his upbringing. He was born between six and seven in the morning, two months premature. The wife of Hogan Campbell, M.P., described him at the age of four as "a lovely child . . . as fat as Trub was at his age."[16]

Once the teenaged George became heir apparent, the matter of his education became paramount and she had perception enough to decide that Dr. Hayter, Bishop of Norwich, installed as the prince's sub-preceptor after Frederick's death, was not "very proper to convey knowledge to children."[17]

George had been raised at the very hub of the opposition to the present administration. Care had to be taken to ensure that his education follow acceptable lines. As a result, the prince's schoolroom became a battlefield for the next four years "with the favor of the future king as the prize of victory."[18]

At the time of Frederick's death, Princes George and Edward were under the tutelage of Dr. Francis Aycough. Frederick's Clerk of the Closet, as preceptor, and Lord North, father of the future prime minister, as governor. Their deputies, who actually did most of the work, were George Lewis Scott, a mathematician and fellow of the Royal Academy, and Andrew Stone, Newcastle's undersecretary of state.

The Pelham Whigs recommended, and the king duly appointed, Dr. Thomas Hayter, Bishop of Norwich, as preceptor and Lord Harcourt, an orthodox Whig, as governor to succeed Aycough and North. Scott and Stone, however, retained their posts.

This arrangement, however, was not destined to last. Within a year Hayter was accusing Scott of "insulting language and personal violence." Harcourt, in turn, accused Stone and Cresset, Princess Augusta's private secretary, of encouraging young George and his brother in Jacobite, Tory ways.

The charges were of sufficient gravity to move George II to appoint an investigative committee early in 1753. To make a long story short, the committee decided the charges were groundless, but Hayter and Harcourt resigned. In their stead, George II appointed as preceptor John Thomas, Bishop of

Peterborough, and as governor Lord Waldegrave, whom the prince was later to describe as "depraved and worthless."

The households settled into something resembling order despite Princess Augusta's misgivings about Stone, whom she felt hardly earned his keep. Scott remained as sub-preceptor until 1755, when the 17-year-old prince got a new one—John Stuart, the third Earl of Bute.

Although Bute leaves the political scene only months after the beginning of the period under discussion, he cannot be ignored or overestimated in his influence on George during his eight years as George's tutor and confidant.

Not only did he do much to shape the prince's intellect and the path he would take when king, he also was instrumental in reshaping the leadership in Parliament that led to the unsteady course of the first few years of the young king's reign.

He was also the target selected by the opposition at home and the dissident colonists on the other side of the Atlantic who were loath to lay the cause of their discontent at the feet of the king.

John Stuart, the third Earl of Bute, was born May 25, 1713, in Edinburgh, Scotland, the son of James, second earl of Bute, and Lady Anne Campbell, one year before the first of the Hanoverian line ascended the throne. He was educated at Eton and in the Netherlands, where he received a degree in civil and public law.

Tall and slim, he was deemed to be very handsome and also proud and pompous "and renowned more than anything else for his handsome legs."[19] At age 23, he was one of 16 Scottish peers elected to the English House of Lords, although he never actually occupied the seat, even though he was re-elected in 1761, 1768 and 1774. The same year he was first elected to the House of Lords, he married Mary, daughter of Edward and Lady Mary Wortley Montagu and, on the death of his father-in-law in 1761, controlled his wife's fortune.

His first honorary title came in 1738, when he was made a Knight of the Thistle, a decoration often used by the Hanoverian kings to reward Scottish nobles who supported the Hanoverian and Protestant cause. The family moved to England in 1745 after the third Jacobite uprising in Scotland.

On a rainy night in Egham in 1747, so the story goes, Frederick, Prince of Wales, and Princess Augusta were prevented from leaving the races by the downpour, and Bute was among those summoned to the royal tent to make up a whist party. From this chance meeting came one of the most historically significant friendships in English or American history.

By 1750, Bute was lord of Frederick's bedchamber and on the death of Frederick his influence over Augusta's household only increased. He busied himself with royal politics, taking part in the negotiations between Leicester House and William Pitt in 1755 against the Duke of Newcastle and in the conferences between Pitt and Newcastle in 1757 that led to their taking office together.

Of even more importance, in 1755 he was named Prince George's sub-preceptor, replacing George Lewis Scott, who had held the post since September, 1749, and the following year was awarded the post of groom of the stole to George.

The 17-year-old prince "was of average intelligence and of more than average intellectual curiosity, but with no experience of the world and intensely lonely."[20] From his earliest childhood he was made conscious of his royal rank. Bute became a father figure to the young prince and—if the rumors are to be believed—something like a husband to Augusta. By the time of his succession in 1760, George constantly sought the earl's approval in everything. "If there was a thought in his head that was not Bute's, he went to the earl for correction."

No one, not even his rather possessive mother, exerted more influence over the prince in all matters, political and personal.

According to Churchill[21] "Ideas that the prince was deliberately indoctrinated with notions of absolutism can be dismissed—the history dispensed by Bute was impeccably Whiggish—but he was taught that his grandfather was a despicable cipher in the power of corrupt ministers."

Chapter 8

The Prince of Wales reportedly received news of his grandfather's death while enjoying an October gallop in the park at Kew. Returning home, his first move was to dispatch a letter to Bute.

Bute had been the prince's guide, counselor and confidant for years, and for all that time both knew George would one day wear the crown. So it is obvious that they had discussed the prince's political future. In 1758, for example, George was writing Bute in terms of "when I mount the throne." [1]

Since the death of his father, George had been brought up at Leicester House, traditional residence of the Prince of Wales, "amid the opposition views of his mother and confidant, the Earl of Bute."[2] Among other things, he was taught that his grandfather "was a despicable cipher in the power of corrupt ministers,"[3] which included, naturally, Pitt and Newcastle, the leaders of Commons.

With his earlier characterizations of both, there is little doubt that the young prince savored the prospect of dismissing them both. But on accession, anticipation and reality came face to face—and reality won.

With the Seven Years War still in progress, and successfully so, George's first moves were cautious. There was no particular unanimity in the Cabinet. For more than three years Pitt had run the war and the Cabinet with a high hand. Despite his genius, or perhaps because of it, Pitt was not the most endearing of men. "For all his genius," as one writer put it succinctly, "He was a man who ruled by fear rather than affection."[4] Demanding, impatient with incompetence, his was a driving personality. But his power was rooted in the English people.

Newcastle, as Pitt's political partner, exercised wide patronage through wealth and connections, "a man of limited intelligence and fussy nature, but of vast territorial and electoral wealth."[5] He possessed landed estates in 13 counties "and could control political influence in proportion."[6] But he was recognized as neither a genius nor endearing.

With the embarassment of riches that came with a year of victories and the heavy tax load required to pay for the seemingly interminable war, a peace movement was growing. While the old George occupied the throne, there was no nucleus powerful enough to attract a peace party as such or to lead such a party in concerted resistance to the Pitt-Newcastle partnership.

With George's accession, the dynamics changed since it was well know that he, Bute and Princess Augusta were in favor of ending the war.

George came to the throne with two objectives in mind—ending the war and transferring the seat of power from Parliament to the throne.

And while it has been argued that neither George nor Bute wanted nor worked for Pitt's resignation from government, their actions would indicate otherwise. Even before the accession, Bute was described a "the most dangerous of Pitt's opponents and it was he who stimulated opinion and the press against the war policy of the minister."[7]

Part of the animosity sprang from the fact that Bute and Pitt were once political allies as part of the Leicester House crowd, supporting Princess Augusta in 1755 against Lord Cumberland and Fox. The alliance came to an end in 1757 when Pitt accepted an appointment in the government of George II with Newcastle as the First Lord of the Treasury following the Braddock fiasco in North America and the loss of Minorca. Even having a Liecester House crony running the ministry was not enough to offset the feeling of betrayal, which gives some indication of the depth of feeling against George II.

According to White, "The young man who came to the throne in 1760 lacked confidence in everything but the wisdom of his friend and tutor, Lord Bute, and the rightness of his own intentions."[8] And on coming into power "The Earl of Bute formed the plan of breaking the phalanx which constituted and supported the ministry, and of securing the independence of the crown," Adolphus wrote in his history published shortly after 1800, a work George III himself described as accurate "as far at least as respected himself."[9]

Within hours of George II's death, it was "clear to all by now that Lord Bute, although not yet a Privy Councilor nor occupying a seat in the Cabinet, was assuming the authority of the King's First Minister."[10]

Within three days, Bute was in the Cabinet and in March of the following year, (1761) he was named Secretary of State for the Northern Department with Pitt remaining as Secretary of State for the Southern Department and Newcastle as First Lord of the Treasury.

With George on the throne, Bute was elevated to privy councilor, groom of the stole and first gentleman of the bedchamber. "Bute, the minister behind the curtain, was now all-powerful at court."[11] Nor were other honors long in coming. In November, he appeared in Commons in his role as the king's first minister. In May, 1762, he succeeded Lord Newcastle as First Lord of the Treasury.

Over those months between accession and mid-1762, there was a great deal of internal conflict since once "the king in name (George) met the king in deed (Pitt), there followed a duel for the throne."[12]

Because of the successful prosecution of the war and management of Parliament by Pitt and Newcastle, George and Bute had to proceed slowly but methodically against them. It took some time to build a coalition in Parliament. "It took seven months of manipulation, of binding the faltering to the king through favors, playing on antipathy to Pitt and Newcastle, to weld a workable majority against them."[13]

Not that George was without allies in his drive for reformation. For nearly 50 years, the Tories had been systematically excluded from positions of power and now the Tory-minded "Country Party" flocked to the support of the new king.

Despite the success of the war, small cracks were beginning to appear in the popular support the Pitt-Newcastle government had enjoyed. It appeared, at least to some, that most of the war's aims had been achieved and continuation was pointless. "It really looks as if we intend to finish the conquest of the world next campaign," Horace Walpole wrote in 1760.[14] "Bute found it only too easy to convert the feeling of weariness into an effective opposition to Pitt."[15]

To others, the cost of the war was an intolerable burden on the populace. It was costing some £6,000,000 to support the land forces and another three and a quarter million for the navy. Funds to support Frederick and his Prussians (some £670,000 a year)[16] along with payments to other assorted German allies cost another two and a half million, an extremely large total for the time.[17]

Another block of Parliamentary support that fell to the crown was about a third of the House of Commons membership that habitually looked to the crown for their "interest," the so-called "Court Party." This group of courtiers, placemen and others supported the king's minister, whoever he might be, "simply because he was the king's minister."[18]

Between the two blocs, George had a workable majority of the 500-member House of Commons but Pitt's popularity with the people was still a matter to be reckoned with. Under George II, Pitt had demanded and been given carte blanche in waging the ongoing Seven Years War. He had even put the new king on notice, through Bute, that he would brook no interference under the new regime.

There followed, for a few months, an uneasy working relationship which came to a head in September, 1761, when Pitt pressed for a declaration of war against Spain, citing intercepted Spanish correspondence that showed Spain intended to join with France under the Bourbon Compact. "Pitt advocated beating the Spanish to the punch and, among other things, seize the annual Spanish gold shipment from the New World."[19]

What Pitt didn't know was that Bute had that year put out peace feelers to France through the Sardinian minister, the Comte de Viry.

Given the opposition by Bute and, therefore, the king, the Cabinet turned down the proposal and on Oct. 5, Pitt resigned. By engineering the vote of "no confidence," the major of the two partners was erased from office, although he left with a peerage as Lord Chatham and a pension. He was succeeded as secretary of state by Lord Egremont.

With Pitt gone, Newcastle became the next target for removal. Henry Fox, longtime Paymaster of the Forces—a post that made him wealthy—was named by George III in 1762 as leader of the House of Commons with the purpose of ushering the peace treaty through Parliament. Newcastle, who was not displeased to see Pitt out of government, soon found his power being curtailed. Particularly damaging was his loss of control over the treasury in May, 1762, to Bute. As George's "hatchet man," Fox put the treasury post to good use, picking off Newcastle supporters through "bribes, irritations or menaces."[20] "Unsupported by the fame of Pitt, the Duke of Newcastle was an easy victim and the administration slid easily into the hands of Lord Bute," Churchill writes.[21]

In January, once its treasure ships were safely in harbor, Spain officially joined with France and the Bute ministry was forced to declare war against the Spanish.

By August of 1762, peace negotiations has reached the point where it became necessary to appoint a British plenipotentiary to Paris, and the job fell to the Duke of Bedford, leader of the "peace at any price" school.[22]

Negotiations were also underway with Spain, and George was reportedly "much hurt" on news that then British fleet had captured Havana which "threatened to delay the conclusion of the treaty with Spain."[23]

As negotiations proceeded with France, reports of Bedford's soft stance on peace conditions were creating problems within the British government. Lord Egremont, Secretary of State for the Southern Department, and his brother-in-law, leader of the House of Commons George Grenville would have to defend the treaty in Parliament despite the fact that they disagreed with Bedford's concessions. Both threatened resignation and Bute was obviously having trouble controlling the situation.

At this point, Bute informed the king he wanted to retire from government service. Passage of the treaty was not the only thing burdening Bute at this point. He was keenly aware of his unpopularity with the general public, otherwise known as the London mob. He was unable to appear in public without being insulted because of his supposed relationship with the queen and now as the perceived author of an unpopular treaty which was seen as being too gracious to the French and Spanish.

In order to forestall Bute's departure, George agreed they needed the devil to do the devil's work and consented to the "desperate expedient" of naming Henry Fox to a seat in the cabinet and as head of the House of Commons. Fox had enriched himself a Paymaster-General of the Forces, had little political influence but was under the patronage of George's uncle, the Duke of Cumberland. He also hated both Pitt and Newcastle and "stood for all that King George had been taught to abhor."[24]

But he was considered devious enough to shepherd the treaty through Parliament and expendable enough to take the criticism and then be thrown back to the sidelines.

A draft of the treaty was received in London in September, 1762, and the signed treaty in November, when even George was taken aback by its concessions to France. George and Bute apparently misread the temper of the House of Commons because, after years of a very expensive war, the treaty was approved in January by a 319-65 vote. Given the one-sided vote, Grenville, although he was considered "inexperienced and untrustworthy," probably could have moved the treaty ratification.

Not long after Fox was able to assure Bute that he had a majority in the House of Commons, Bute began to display signs of paranoia. He recommended to the king that the Duke of Devonshire—the king's chamberlain and a member of the Privy Council—be invited to a meeting to review the terms of the final treaty. Devonshire declined the invitation, which Bute interpreted as a sign that Devonshire was plotting his overthrow in concert with Newcastle and Cumberland.

As a result, George took the unusual step of dismissing Devonshire from the Privy Council, whereupon his relatives also resigned from government. "Dismissal from the Privy Council was rare," according to Brooke. "The last case was that of Lord George Sackville in 1760 for disobedience of military orders at the battle of Minden."

With the treaty approved, Fox proved harder to be rid of than anticipated. He embarked on a purge of Newcastle and all his followers. In the words of Horace Walpole, "A more severe political persecution never raged."[25] "The first time he (Newcastle) left office (in 1757) most of his followers rightly expected him to return and stuck to him; the second time (in 1762) they as rightly foresaw that he would stay out, and many of them left him."[26] By the end of January, Bute was writing the king that "The angel Gabriel could not at present govern this country but by means too long practiced and such as my soul abhors."[27]

As much as he detested the man, Bute recommended Fox as his successor as Prime Minister. Fox declined, but recommended "meek and submissive" Grenville who was on the other hand also a master of finance and Pitt's brother-in-law. Bute resigned in April, and Grenville was named first minister. Only four months later, after Grenville and the king have a falling out over the appointment of the Keeper of the Privy Purse, Bute opened negotiations for the return of Pitt to government. Pitt's demands, however, proved more than either George or Bute were willing to cede, and Grenville was asked to remain in office.

Later in the year, Bute left London for Harrogate. Although he no longer held any official position, his shadow hung over the political scene for some time to come, first as the king's continuing favorite and, later, as a bogey man.

Chapter 9

Whether the Treaty of Paris represented an end or a beginning depends on the point of view. "The British triumph of 1763 marked the end, not the glorious beginning, of an era"[1] says one author, but to another it "opened a new era in the relationship between the colonies and the mother country."[2] But beginning or end, the year 1763 was a definite point of changing direction in the current of British-American history.

Provisions of the treaty were not universally accepted by the British, although they were weary of the protracted and expensive war. Pitt, now out of power, thought that John Russell, the Fourth Duke of Bedford and Lord Bute's principal negotiator, far too lenient and "vehemently denounced the treaty as undermining the safety of the realm" while Bedford feared that England, by taking took much of the globe, "would be in perpetual danger from European coalitions and attacks by dissatisfied nations."[3].

Bedford was the "strongest among ministers for ending the war,"[4] while Pitt contended the government would find no "secure or permanent peace until France and Spain were placed at a lasting disadvantage."[5] His protests were to no avail, however, and, considering the unqualified defeat suffered by the Bourbon powers and their allies, generous terms were agreed to by England.

Among the examples of weakness in the treaty cited by Churchill[6] was the return of Guadeloupe—"the richest prize of the war"—to the French. He further notes that its monetary value prompted the English to consider keeping it and returning Canada. Had Pitt been at the negotiating table, England probably would have kept both. Given Bedford's appeasing state of mind, however, the choice had to be made. It became one of the most widely discussed portions of the treaty.

Arguments for and against the retention of Canada instead of Guadeloupe are worth looking at closely since, at least to the North American colonists, they came to represent British attitudes and intentions toward them. As the Earl of Hardwicke wrote the Duke of Newcastle, then prime minister, in 1762: "It will come now to be a more grave question whether you should restore to France all her Sugar-Colonies, or a great part of Canada."

Guadeloupe or Canada, that was the choice France had maneuvered England into and seemingly everyone was willing to offer his advice. The issue spawned a flurry of pamphlets and letters supporting both sides. For his part, Hardwicke continued his letter to the Prime Minister by pointing out that Canada's climate was cold and unfruitful, that it cost France more to maintain than it produced, that it was destined to remain sparsely populated "in centuries to come" and, unless the French inhabitants were removed, it would be necessary to maintain an army there "to keep them in subjection."[7]

France's sugar islands, on the other hand, were fertile, could be easily populated and defended, would provide a good market for English manufactures and besides, 'The sugar trade is a most profitable one . . ."[8]

Many of Hardwicke's contemporaries shared his view of

Canada as a rather worthless piece of real estate. Some added a consideration borne of the long-standing apprehension over colonial independence. By leaving a potentially dangerous neighbor on the colonies' borders, they argued, colonial dependence would be assured.

A year earlier, the Duke of Bedford also wrote to Newcastle on the subject. "Indeed, my lord, I don't know whether the neighborhood of the French to our North American colonies was not the greatest security for their dependence on the mother country, which I feel will be slighted by them when their apprehension of the French is removed."[9]

Nor was this feeling restricted to the western side of the English Channel. In 1763, the Comte de Vergennes, French ambassador to Constantinople when the treaty was signed, concurred with Bedford. "Delivered of a neighbor whom they always feared, your other colonies will soon discover that they stand no longer in need of your protection. You will call on them toward supporting the burthen which they have helped bring upon you, they will answer by shaking off all dependence."[10]

Not that the presence of the French might help keep the English colonists in line was a new idea. A Swedish botanist named Peter Kalm, writing in 1748, maintained it was "of great advantage to the crown of England that the North American colonies are near a country under the government of the French, like Canada. There is reason to believe that the king never was earnest in his attempts to expel the French from their possessions there; though it might have been done with little difficulty."[11]

Since Kalm was traveling in the colonies, and since there were few British officials in the colonies, it isn't hard to imagine where this "reason to believe" came from. It sprang at least in part from the return that year of Fort Louisburg, one of France's major strongholds, captured in 1745 by New Englanders in King George's War (1744-48) "and its restoration came to New England as the sorest affront which it had ever received at the hands of the home government."[12] The French had started construction of the Cape Breton Island fortress in 1713 and completed at an estimated cost of 30,000,000 livres.

Among the more cogent pamphlets urging retention of Canada instead of Guadeloupe was published in London in the spring of 1760 under the rather lengthy title of "The Interest of Great Britain Considered, With Regard to Her Colonies and the Acquisition of Canada and Guadeloupe." Its authors were Benjamin Franklin, Pennsylvania's then colonial agent, and Richard Jackson, London agent for both Connecticut and Pennsylvania as well as a member of Parliament and private secretary to Lord Grenville.

In their pamphlet, the pair took more pains to puncture the anti-Canada arguments than to refute the pro-Guadeloupe contentions. They started by pointing out the difficulties of maintaining peace along a 1,500-mile frontier where the residents "are generally the refuse of both nations."[13] The choice of words would indicate Jackson's London view rather than Franklin's colonial outlook.

The writers also noted that frontier wars have a way of spreading to involve their mother countries. England and France had recognized the reverse of this truism 75 years earlier when they pledged themselves to neutrality in the Americas in the Treaty of Whitehall (1686).[14]

Retention of Canada, so Franklin and Jackson reasoned, would also go far toward solving the Indian question. With no other Europeans around to incite them or furnish them arms and ammunition, there would be no doubt of their living peacefully with the English "if we treat them with common justice."[15] Gone also would be the necessity of defending a long frontier in the event of renewal of hostilities with France.

In the matter of commercial value, the authors argued that Canada really didn't suffer by comparison with

Guadeloupe. Trade with the West Indies was at a standstill, they maintained, and the addition of Guadeloupe would not help the situation significantly. Commerce with the northern colonies, however, "is not only greater, but yearly increasing with the increase of the people."

Cognizance was also taken of the independence question and the solution being proposed—returning Canada to France so the continued presence of the French would keep the colonies dependent. As far as independence was concerned, had not the colonies demonstrated their inability of united action against the French and Indians "who were perpetually harassing their settlements, burning their villages, and murdering their people." How then could they unite against their mother country "which protects and encourages them, with which they have so many connexions and ties of blood, interest, and affection, and which, it is well known, they all love much more than they love one another?"

Addressing themselves to the second point, they cautioned that returning Canada to France to assure colonial dependence could well have the opposite effect. This course would make England responsible for any future deaths since it would indicate to the French "that the horrid barbarities they perpetuate with the Indians on our colonies are agreeable to us." Colonists could hardly feel kindly toward the nation that left them in such danger. "Is not this the most likely means of driving them into the arms of the French, who can invite them by an offer of security, their own government chooses not to afford them?"

While put forward as the thoughts of thoroughly loyal English subjects, the pamphlet made clear several points dear to the colonists' hearts and probably attributable to Franklin. In speaking of the French and Indian attacks, it argued that where frontier people owe and pay allegiance to the mother country "there they have a right to look for protection. No political proposition is better established than this."

Later, although terming a union of the colonies "impossible," an indirect warning was included. Unity against England would be impossible in the absence of "the most grievous tyranny and oppression." Because of their close ties with the colonies, Franklin and Jackson can be reasonably supposed to reflect a majority of colonial thinking when they said "While the government is mild and just, while important civil and religious rights are secure, such subjects will be dutiful and obedient."

And in the best Poor Richard tradition, they added this homily: "The waves do not rise but when the wind blows."

Those advocating the retention of Canada for all the reasons put forth by the colonists were joined by many of those in the English sugar trade, which was tightly controlled as regards its preferred position vis-à-vis sugar produced by non-English plantations. Their view was that addition of the Guadeloupe sugar crop to that already in the closed economic system would depress sugar prices and profits.

One other provision of the treaty deserves special note, particularly in view of the disturbance raised among the New England colonies by the Quebec Act 11 years later (1774). Among other things, the act guaranteed Canadians the right to practice Catholicism. "One of the peculiar charms of New England," Miller quotes the Rev. Jonathan Mayhew, [16] "was that a Roman Catholic was rarely seen and thereby the Saints were preserved from all contamination."

But the Yankee clerics were apparently a little slow in their reactions, since in the Treaty of Paris "His Britannic Majesty, on his side, agrees to grant liberty of the Catholic religion to the inhabitants of Canada." [17]

The treaty was met with a considerable uproar, not only from the man in the street but also from the occupants of the benches in Parliament.

Pitt "vehemently denounced the treaty as undermining the safety of the realm"[18] and he further pointed out that it totally ignored the interests and contributions of Prussia and Frederick the Great.

After a long and bitter debate, the provisions of the treaty were approved by a 5-to-1 margin.

As the first "world war," the Seven Years War had involved the common people and their commercial prosperity as none before it. Great Britain's efforts had been headed by a great war leader now out of power, in ill health and a member of a rather small opposition group. To make matters worse, the treaty was "delivered to the nation at the hands of a detested Scotchman who was suspected of having poisoned the mind of an innocent young price, not to mention seducing his mother."[19]

The victory prompted the first political bloodbath of the new king's reign, with the heavy hand of government turning against those who voted in opposition to the king and his favorite in the so-called "Massacre of the Pelhamite Innocents." The king "was at last able to expend all the hoarded venom of his embittered youth."[20] Among the adherents of the Duke of Newcastle, nobles were stricken from the lists of office holders and benefices. Horace Walpole, in his memoirs, relates that even "old servants who had retired . . . were rigorously hunted out and deprived of their livelihood."[21]

But the Pelhamites were not the only victims of the unpopular treaty. Bute himself became a victim. Not long after the treaty was passed, Bute "laboring under the double stigma of being a Scotchman and the author of the treaty of 1763, retired from English politics, declaring as he surrendered the seals that 'fifty pounds a year and bread and water were luxury to what I suffer'."[22]

Chapter 10

Finally, we reach 1763, which was to have been the starting point for this conversation in the first place.

The young George III, obstinate, reform minded, has been on the throne nearly three years. England's major protagonists—France and Spain—have been reduced to near impotency. His domestic irritants—Pitt and Newcastle—have been removed from government. But his more trusted advisor for more than a decade, Lord Bute, has also left office—although he remained in close consultation with the king for some time—a circumstance, as we shall see, that had its own political ramifications.

All wars are unfortunate, especially for the losers, and the Seven Years War was no exception. As the world's first "World War," it cost the principal loser—France—the profitable subcontinent of India, left her with only a toehold in North America and heaped an additional financial burden on an already overburdened population.

Spain, which became an ally of France very late in the conflict through the Family Compact uniting their Bourbon rulers, could hardly be termed a loser. Although she lost the Floridas to England, France made good the loss by giving her the Louisiana Territory. England also returned the Philippines and Havana, so, while the Spanish came out of the war poorer in coin, they lost little in the way of possessions.

Austria, Russia, Sweden and Saxony—France's other allies—also emerged from the war with little to show for their efforts but their casualty lists and depleted treasuries.

Prussia, England's sole ally in the war, also had a long casualty list after signing a treaty that was "a status quo in every particular."[1] Frederick the Great had one consolation, however. Because English aid had taken the form of money rather than troops, Prussia was in better financial condition than the other combatants.

To the big winner—England—the war brought an empire so vast that some of the more exultant English were led to refer to the antique Romans as "triflers to us."[2] Her ships commanded the high seas. The wealth of India was hers as was North America from the St. Lawrence on the north to the Gulf of Mexico on the south.

"England . . . defended and nourished by the sea, rode it everywhere in triumph."[3]

But the Treaty of Paris was not an unalloyed blessing. The liberality of the terms shocked even King George and the Pitt element of government was outraged. Even some segments of the general public, weary as they were of the seemingly endless war, were less than thrilled when the details of the treaty were made known.

One of the major problems was that the war had left England with a national debt of between £122,603,366 and £140,000,000. (Higginbotham p.34, and Mahan p. 323, quote the low figure; Fuller Vol. II, p. 272, and Degler, p. 76, agree on £130,000,000; J.C. Miller p. 82, and White P. 93, quote the high figure) Whatever the figure, it was close to double what it had been before the war, a circumstance that was to have far-reaching consequences. In fact, the conflict had "loaded every state of Europe, save Prussia, with such a national debt as they have never yet been able to liquidate."[4] The months surrounding the negotiations that led to the Treaty of Paris, first begun in secret, were a period of political countercurrents for the king, his ministers and for the negotiators from Europe. Neither wanted to appear too anxious to end the war lest their negotiating positions be weakened. On the other hand, the English negotiators hesitated to push too hard for concessions for fear that they would create lasting animosities that could result in further hostilities.

With the treaty shepherded through the House of Commons by Henry Fox using, some would claim, very devious methods, including "bribes, irritations or menaces."[5], Bute tendered his resignation as prime minister.

The next seven years were a period of almost continuous change as George searched for a prime minister with a firm enough hand and political clout enough to steer the ship of state in the direction he wanted it to go. It has given rise to innumerable studies, opposing theories and explanations because it was the era that brought about the birth of a new nation on the eastern side of the Atlantic.

By this time, Bute was afraid to appear in public unattended. As a Scotsman, as the king's favorite appointed over men of more experience and as the supposed paramour of the king's mother, he was thoroughly disliked, thanks in no small part to the anti-government press that kept all three points before its readers.

Coming to the conclusion that the country was so unmanageable that "the Angel Gabriel could not at present govern the country, but by means too long practic'd and such as my soul abhor,"[6] Bute was determined to leave office, if not leave politics.

Apparently renouncing his high-minded aspirations for the young king and country, Bute recommended Henry Fox—a man unpalatable to both—as his successor as a knave to lead a country of knaves after overtures to William Pitt came to nothing.

George was reluctant but, if that was what Bute thought best, he was willing to go along. Fox was offered the leadership post. It was the time, the king decided, to "call in bad men to govern bad men."[7]

Knave though he was, Fox was not dumb or really courageous. He declined the offer on the grounds of his and his wife's health and suggested instead George Grenville, who was first lord of the admiralty at the time. Fox was also well content to line his pockets in his present position as Paymaster to the Services.

Grenville was well connected politically and had been serving in one office or another since being elected to the House of Commons in 1741 from the borough of Buckingham, a minute borough with only 13 electors, all thoroughly under the control of his uncle, Richard, Viscount Cobham.

He was a brother-in-law to William Pitt, although he was on the other side in promoting the Treaty of Paris that Pitt so strongly opposed.

After the fall of Newcastle in 1762 and the accession of Bute, Grenville was named Secretary of State for the Northern Department, where he teamed with another brother-in-law, Lord Egremont, who was Secretary of State for the Southern Department.

When it was learned that Bute had opened secret peace negotiations without consulting his cabinet, Grenville opposed the move, earning him a demotion to First Lord of the Admiralty.

In accepting the leadership post, Grenville appreciated the fact that he had little to feel secure about in his new position. The other members of the government had been chosen by Bute and Fox and he was equally aware of ongoing negotiations to lure Pitt back from his Olympian retreat before he even had a chance to warm his chair as the king's first minister.

In one of the more ironic twists in the tale of George's early days on the throne, his uncle, the Duke of

Cumberland—known as the "Butcher" for his treatment of the Scotch[8] during the Bonnie Prince Charlie uprising and "the dreaded ogre of his childhood"—was to become in his last days the king's most trusted advisor and the go-between with Pitt as George sought to replace one man he didn't like—Grenville—with a man he liked even less—Pitt.

The duke was even to leave a horticultural footnote in history. A flower was named after him to mark his success at the battle of Culloden against the Scotch. In England it is known as Sweet William, but in Scotland it is known as the Stinking Billy.[9]

Negotiations with Pitt apparently broke down when Pitt demanded a purge of those who supported the Treaty of Paris, a sort of counter purge to that that swept out the treaty's opponents about a year earlier—a condition George could not accept.

With his options vanished, George had little choice to support Grenville—much as he would have liked to replace him.

The first storm of the Grenville administration broke within weeks of its inception—a domestic row brought on by John Wilkes, a member of parliament and publisher of the anti-government *North Briton* periodical. In the infamous issue No. 45, Wilkes attacked the tax and insinuated that the king had lied in a speech before parliament defending the Cider Tax Act.

Grenville regained some favor with Bute by speaking in favor of a Cider Tax, put forward by Bute and his Chancellor of the Exchequer, as a means of reducing the country's national debt. The proposal called for a tax of four shilling per hogshead to add to the existing beer tax "while the land tax was still to stand at its top rate of four shillings."[10] Sir Francis Dashwood was widely believed not to understand the legislation he was proposing and Grenville, in supporting the measure, reaped ridicule in the House. After prompting riots in the West Country, the measure was soundly defeated.

While the Cider Tax Act was in itself a minor piece of legislation, the subsequent arrest of Wilkes for seditious libel along with everyone else connected with preparation of the publication produced two long-lasting results. A jury found for Wilkes and his fellow defendants and entered a judgment of £4,000 against George Montague Dunk, Lord Halifax, George's secretary of state, and so was born the legal principal of freedom of the press.

The second effect came in the ruling that the so-called "Dunk Warrant," a piece of paper that, according to one legal scholar, "may be the single most important warrant in the history of Anglo-American law."[11] Issued by Halifax, the warrant called for the arrest of everyone connected with No. 45 along with their papers and that they be brought before Halifax "to be examined concerning the premises and further dealt with according to law." The warrant was dated just three days after the North Briton appeared—April 26, 1763.

More than 40 persons were arrested under Halifax' warrant and many brought suit against Halifax for their arrest.

"The judges who heard the cases reasoned that warrant invalid because it swept too broadly—both because it left the officers with discretion regarding whom, precisely, they should arrest and because it allowed the seizure of all their papers," Sklansky wrote. These principles reappear in the American Constitution's prohibition against "unreasonable searches and seizures."

Wilkes was turned out of parliament, re-elected, turned out a second time and later became Lord Mayor of London.

Even while distracted with the long-running Wilkes affair, Grenville still had the state of Great Britain's economy to worry about.

Grenville, according to Howard, "was an honest man, too independent to be counted among the 'king's friends,' but of small talent." [12] Honest or not, of small talent or not, he was unscrupulous enough and smart enough to take advantage of the king's quandary.

He insisted on an end to Bute's behind-the-scenes meddling. He disputed with the king over personal appointments—including replacement of the court painter and the naming of Bute's successor as Keeper of the Privy Purse—but while keeping a tight rein on royal expenditures, he proceeded to do very well for himself and his family.

Grenville was credited with being a master of finance but to the king he had "the mind of a clerk in a counting house."[13] Not that George was unmindful of the tremendous national debt and the need for economy, even in his own household. Virtually every financial transaction came under scrutiny, ranging from the maids of honor's allowance for breakfast to the allowances to his brothers, Edward of York and Prince William.

To the horror of Pitt, the army was reduced from 120,000 to 30,000 men and naval upkeep was trimmed drastically. A dozen years later, the effects of these economies would make themselves felt on the far side of the Atlantic.

In 1764, Grenville turned his accounting-house mind toward finding a way to increase the country's revenues from the North American colonies both by enforcing the legislation already on the books and by new revenue measures.

"What Grenville tried to do in America raised a storm that blew for 20 years, and at the end left an irreparable trail of ruin"[14]

As for raising revenue from the American colonies, the idea was not original with Grenville. As early as 1728, and again in 1739, Sir William Keith, governor of Pennsylvania, had proposed a similar measure. The idea was advanced again in 1744 by Lieutenant Governor Clarke of New York to Governor Clinton and in 1755 Governors (William) Shirley (of Massachusetts, 1753-56) and (Robert) Dinwiddie (of Virginia, 1751-56) had suggested a similar measure, but any consideration was put on the back burner because of the impending war with France.

During the war, it was not deemed expedient to press the matter while the active support of the colonies was needed.

With the hostilities at an end, however, Grenville put the idea into action by sponsoring a series of acts intended to raise a revenue and clamp down on smugglers, starting with the Sugar Act of 1764 and the Currency Act of the same year.

These two acts were like boulders among a sea of pebbles that had been irritating the colonists for a long time. There were the Navigation Acts, with their ever-increasing restrictions on trade and manufacture. There was the conversion of colonies from proprietary or charter to royal, with the resulting loss on any part in selecting a governor.

And then there was the "suspending clause."

Since the earliest days, most colonial charters provided for a legislature or assembly of some sort to pass laws governing the colony, and subject to the approval of the governor. Naturally, no laws were to be passed that were in contravention of existing English law and so were subject to review by the Privy Council in England.

This review process might take months at best and years at worst. Should a provincial piece of legislation be disapproved by the Privy Council, it was declared null and void as of the date the governor was informed of its disapproval. Massachusetts set a three-year limit of the length of time the Privy Council had to disallow a law, while Pennsylvania set the limit at six months after receipt by the Privy Council.

Six months may have been pushing matters, given the four-step inspection received by each piece of legislation. It first went to the legal counsel of the Lords Commissioners for Trade and Plantations—more commonly known as the Board of Trade; then to the board, then went to a committee of the Privy Council, the Committee on Plantation Affairs, and then to the full Privy Council. Given the volume of legislation generated by the North American colonies, three years might have been more realistic than six months.

In the early 1750s, not by act of Parliament but rather by royal instructions to royal governors, it was decreed that any colonial legislation not approved by the Privy Council was invalid. As set forth, this meant that any colonial laws that drew disapproval were invalid from their inception, regardless of how long it might take for the council to make up its mind. In addition, each new piece of colonial legislation that amended in any way an act previously approved by the Privy Council had to contain a clause specifying to that condition or the governor was instructed not to approve it.

Colonial legislatures naturally protested on both philosophical and practical grounds. Not only did the suspending clause undermine the colonies' ability to govern themselves, it was also argued the impossibility of being governed for a couple of years only to find that the law was invalid from day one.

The North American colonies chafed, but grew, under what they saw as increasing interference, but the Sugar Act and Currency Act were a magnitude larger than what had gone before.

The Sugar Act of 1764, as adopted, was a revision of the Sugar Act of 1733—otherwise known as the Molasses Act or the American Revenue Act—which had been intended to stop the American colonists from trading with the French Caribbean islands through a prohibitively high tariff of sixpence a gallon on foreign molasses.

The original act created little controversy in the colonies because—thanks primarily to the royal government's attitude of benign neglect and only perfunctory efforts to collect the tax—it was generally ignored. Smuggling was easier that a prolonged legal and philosophical battle over what was or was not constitutional.

A merchant who had lived in the colonies for more than two decades explained the economics to Parliament—excess lumber and other colonial products were bought by the French and paid for with molasses; the molasses went back to New England, where it was distilled into rum; the rum was then carried to Africa and other ports where it bought "gold dust, elephants' teeth and slaves for the sugar planters."[15]

Under the new legislation, the duty would be cut in half, thereby it was reasoned there would less temptation to smuggle. In addition, the act forbade the importation of foreign rum, added taxes to a number of other items previously untaxed and vested customs service officers with additional powers of collection.

What set the act apart from all previous acts concerning colonial trade was its intent—"improving the revenue of this kingdom." It went on further to state that "it is just and necessary, that a revenue be raised." (Text) Thus the Sugar Act of 1764 became the first parliamentary measure intended from the very outset to tax the colonies for revenue rather than for the regulation of trade.

It should be recalled that the Seven Years War—or in America the French and Indian War—had just concluded. There were thousands of British troops still on this side of the Atlantic. London was convinced that at least part of them had to remain to ensure the peace and, incidentally, enforce the various royal edicts and parliamentary legislation. It was also felt that it was only fitting that the colonies contribute to the upkeep of those troops.

In May, 1764, readers of the Boston *News Letter* learned that Parliament had determined that in passing the Sugar Act "they had the power to lay such a tax on the colonies" even though the colonists had no representation in Parliament.[16] Reid makes the point that Parliament, in making a conscious decision in the matter, considered the constitutionality of colonial taxation even before the colonists raised the question.

Grenville, in leading the debate in Commons, stated clearly that the Sugar Act was intended to "raise the revenue in America for defending itself."[17] He inquired whether there were any in the house who questioned the right of Parliament to levy taxes on the colonies. Virginia's agent, reporting on the debates, noted that the "members interested in the plantations expressed great surprise that a doubt of that nature could ever exist."[18]

As a corollary, the debate became yet another stage for the ongoing argument about Parliamentary versus royal authority. One speaker complained that royal instructions were going to the colonial governors with the force and effect of law though they did not originate in Parliament.

This was a controversy that had been ongoing for several years. Benjamin Franklin, in London as agent for Pennsylvania in 1759, reported a conversation with Lord Granville, then president of the Privy Council, that "The King in Council is *the Legislator* of the Colonies; and when his Majesty's Instructions come there they are the *Law of the Land* . . . and as such *ought to be obeyed*.[19]

The Sugar Act debates are significant, Reid maintains, "because, though everyone was in agreement, the constitutional issue was nevertheless raised—and dismissed."[20]

Colonial reaction was not long in coming—with that perennial malcontent Massachusetts leading the way. There were protests in New York and Pennsylvania, along with Massachusetts, where distillers and merchants were most directly affected by the impact on their businesses.

Only days after the published notice, Boston voters instructed the lower house of the Massachusetts General Court to question the levying of taxes on a people when the people are not represented in the body levying the tax. If "taxes are laid upon us in any shape without our having a legal representation where they are laid," the resolution argued, it would undermine "our British privileges."

In October, the New York House of the General Assembly echoed the same point in a petition to George III. The New Yorkers maintained that taxes levied by a governmental body in which they were not represented were as unconstitutional as taxes levied by royal prerogative without the consent of any legislative body.

Colonists were far from original in making their "no taxation without representation" argument. It was used at the time of Henry VIII some 200 years before resulting in Chester and Durham gaining actual representation in the House[21] and it had been heard in Ireland "for generations."[22]

While the argument bore fruit for Chester and Durham, it wasn't any more successful for the North American colonists than it was for the Irish.

Another distinguishing characteristic of legislation adopted by the Grenville administration in the year following the Treaty of Paris was parliament's intention to enforce the tax collections.

It was a second provision of the act that created the most problems for the colonists—parliament's obvious intention that the era of salutary neglect was over and this time the act would be enforced. As part of that enforcement effort, vice-admiralty courts were given new powers, a super vice-admiralty court was created in Halifax, Nova Scotia, that had jurisdiction from Newfoundland to the Floridas. In addition, all commanders of British ships-of-war in American waters were deputized as customs house officers "with the usual share in the contraband and confiscated cargoes."[23]

Vice admiralty courts were nothing new either in Europe or in England, where they had been functioning since the 14th Century. Established initially to deal with such seagoing problems as piracy and naval discipline, proceedings were held without a jury, with a crown-appointed judge hearing the evidence and rendering a verdict.

By the 1600s, they had been established in the principal seaports of the American colonies which, in effect, meant all the colonies, and their powers and jurisdiction grew over the years. In 1722, for example, parliament adopted a criminal code covering the felling of white pines, which were to be harvested only for use in His Majesty's Navy. Under the code, the Surveyor-General of the King's Woods in America was authorized to seize "any illegally felled white pine trees or masts or logs cut from them, and sue for the forfeiture in the admiralty court of the colony in which the trees were felled."[24]

Under Grenville's new legislation, vice-admiralty courts were further charged with enforcing customs regulations and prosecuting criminal charges for smuggling, with a built-in financial incentive for a guilty finding.

In the Halifax admiralty court, common legal principals were reversed. Regardless of where a ship might be seized on allegations of smuggling, the defendant was required to travel to Halifax for the trial, he was denied a jury, he was required to post a bond for the value of the confiscated ship and cargo and obliged to prove his innocence before a judge imported from England. If he failed to appear, his guilt was presumed confessed.

In the unlikely event that the defendant won the case, however, he was not entitled to any costs if the judge felt there was probable cause for the complaint nor was the person making the seizure subject to any legal action on the part of the defendant.

As an added feature guaranteed to irk the colonists, all land bound customs officers were armed with "general writs of assistance." They were blank search warrants, allowing the officers to enter and search any premises at any time and on any pretext without specifying what they were looking for. The writs also required that any local law enforcement agency assist them with their search.

It didn't take long for the colonists to realize that the admiralty courts could not only prosecute but also persecute, although to parliament it seemed the only way to avoid sympathetic colonial juries who often returned verdicts in favor of the defendant despite the evidence.

Memorials from the colonies attacked the Sugar Act from every direction. They argued that maintaining a standing army in peacetime—which the act was to help finance—was unconstitutional. They questioned who the army was to protect the colonies from, now that France had been evicted from Canada.

They questioned the right of the king or parliament to levy taxes on them when they were not represented in government. If either could impose a tax without the colonists' consent, it was obviously an arbitrary exercise of power not countenanced by the English constitution.

"If taxes are laid upon us in any shape without our having legal representation where they are laid, are we not reduced from the character of free subjects to the miserable state of tributary slaves?" James Otis of Massachusetts asked in his *Rights of the British Colonies*.[25] Several of the colonial agents in London were chastised by the colonial assemblies for their silence on the subject when the act was under consideration by parliament.

The other shoe fell with the Currency Act that could have dealt a death blow to all colonial trade.

For some 40 years, the colonists had been trying various means to promote trade. In the aftermath of the South Sea Bubble, discussed in connection with Georgia, depression hit England and made its effect felt in the colonies. By 1721, trade in Philadelphia had nearly stopped, money was scarce. The problem, according to merchant Thomas Griffitts was "The want of some proper medium for currency."[26] While gold and silver were preferable, both were as scarce in Pennsylvania as in any other colony. In 1723, the Pennsylvania Assembly passed a money act allowing the issuance of £15,000 in bills of credit. Between 1723 and 1739, the Assembly had adopted four such measures for a total of more than £86,000.

Unlike legal tender, bills of credit were in effect loans at five percent interest from the colonial government to individuals who mortgaged their property in order to secure the loans. Considering that the loans were £12 at a minimum and seldom amounted to more than £300, it is obvious that the participation was widespread.

Four more currency measures during the French and Indian War boosted the total in paper currency to £185,000, but there was a difference. Those issues were to be repaid by a general tax on all landed estates in the colony, making the currency some of the first in America to be backed by the taxing power of the issuer.

But Pennsylvania was well behind Virginia in the amount of paper currency issued. During the French and Indian War she had issued £250,000 in paper.[27]

Rather than try to wrestle with the many forms of paper being circulated in the colonies, rather than try to find a common relationship with the English pound sterling, parliament took the easy way out by banning the whole lot.

In the Currency Act of 1764, Grenville was revisiting plowed ground because what it did was extend the prohibition against paper currency that had been in effect in New England since 1751.

As bad as the Sugar Act and the Currency Act were, they were only a preamble to Grenville's biggest blunder, the Stamp Act of 1765.

Chapter 11

If there is one parliamentary act that made separation almost inevitable, the Stamp Act of 1765 was it.

What came later may have increased the temperature; the Stamp Act lit the fire. It accomplished what none before it had. Until now, the various parliamentary acts had affected the various colonies in differing degrees. But the Stamp Act was universal. It hit everyone all up and down the coast

"Grenville's argument that the tax bore equally on rich and poor only made it hated by the many as well as the few." [1]

Under terms of the act, "every skin or piece of vellum or parchment, or sheet or piece of paper" on which virtually anything was written had to have a duty stamp attached. These ranged in cost from one-half penny a sheet for any pamphlet or newspaper printed on a half sheet to £10 for a legal license to practice in court or to act as a notary public.

With notable thoroughness, the act even provided for a duty of one shilling for a deck of playing cards and 10 shillings for a pair of dice.

As previously mentioned, a similar tax was one of a package adopted in England during the Seven Years War to finance the nation's military campaigns as well as its subsidy to Prussia. One of the most unpopular was the land tax of four shillings on the pound of valuation, a tax most opposed naturally by the landed interests.

Because the gentry as well as the general public felt they were already overburdened, the proposed Cider Tax prompted riots and the threat of parliamentary revolt among the "cider country" members and an additional half-penny on a pint of porter brought an outcry from the lower echelon.

Those of a calculating turn of mind figured the national debt was £18 per person per year in England but only 18 shillings in the colonies. [2]

Grenville, with his counting-house clerk's mind, calculated that it would cost some £200,000[3] a year to maintain 10,000 royal troops in North America. Of that amount, he further calculated, a Stamp Act similar to the one in force in England should produce some £60,000[4].

His arithmetic may have been correct, but his political sensitivity—and that of parliament as a whole—was fatally askew. Why, supporters argued, should our North American colonists, who were so proud to acknowledge themselves as English subjects, object to paying a tax that was, by one estimate, producing as much as one half the country's domestic revenue?[5] Acording to White, the amount collected domestically was some £100,000 a year.[6]

While the Stamp Act might have been "a justifiable act of sovereign authority carried through by an impeccable lawyer,"[7] from a political standpoint it proved to be an unmitigated disaster.

One aspect that made it a disaster was that it fell most heavily on the more prosperous—the merchants and lawyers—and therefore the more conservative segments of the population, that very strata that had been the government's strongest supporters in the colonies. The merchants understood the power of money and the lawyers understood the legalities. Equally as important, it helped bridge the gap between the levels of society that naturally existed then as now. Parliament unwittingly created an alliance it could not resist and even created sympathy at home.

Parliament member Edmund Burke, one of the colonies' staunchest defenders, put his finger on the difference between what is legal and what is humane. The question, according to Burke, was "not what a lawyer tells me I may do, but what humanity, reason and justice tells me I ought to do."[8]

Grenville also gave the colonists a year's notice that the stamp act was coming by informing parliament in 1764 that such a measure would be introduced at its next session, which provided the colonists a year to lodge their complaints and air their opposition—all of which went unheeded. In giving the advance notice, he also offered the colonists time to propose an alternative.

If "they thought any other mode of taxation more convenient to them, and made any proposition which should carry the appearance of equal efficiency with the stamp duty, he would give it all due consideration."[9]

Given the seeming acquiescence of the colonial agents in London and the lack of any alternative proposals from overseas, Grenville and parliament can't be faulted too much for failing to predict the colonial reaction. Even such an eminent observer as Franklin did not. He was, in fact, "ready to recommend various of his friends in America as stamp collectors—a position that promised three hundred pounds a year."[10] He even fleetingly thought about taking such a post himself and his son did.

But the protests were there—petitions, memorials and addresses from Massachusetts, Rhode Island, Connecticut, New York and Virginia. Somewhat unexpectedly, they were joined in their objections by Massachusetts Gov. Francis Bernard and Lt. Gov. Thomas Hutchinson, who was to become Bernard's successor.

Some made the argument that the more money siphoned away from the colonies in the form of taxes and the more colonial trade was restricted, the less the colonists would have to spend on English imports. That line of reasoning fell on deaf ears as did arguments about the constitutionality of taxation without representation. Hadn't parliament already considered the constitutional question during the Sugar Act debates?

For Massachusetts in particular, the prospect of new taxes couldn't have come at a worse time. In January of 1765, the colony found itself on the verge of financial panic. Several of the major shipping companies had closed, thousands of men were out of work. Farmers were still recovering from the drought of the preceding summer only to find no market for their wheat and the general population was recuperating from the smallpox outbreak.

At the same time, Massachusetts, like the other colonies, was distracted in trying to sort its way through the implications of the Sugar Act and Currency Act.

Needless to say, they were in no condition financially, philosophically or emotionally to be sympathetic to any arguments about the overall good of the British empire. As winter moved into spring and a vote in parliament on the Stamp Act neared, apprehension grew.

In the normal course of events, residents from different colonies were in written contact with each other. Relatives wrote relatives, businessmen wrote businessmen, acquaintances wrote acquaintances. And, of course, matters of colonial politics as well as matters bearing on the colony's relations with the mother country were natural matters for discussion.

The dire economic impact of the Sugar and Currency Acts, however, rose above the level of casual conversation between individuals. It became a grave matter at the highest level, and so the acts brought about a quasi-official means of inter-colonial communications—the circular letter generated by committees of correspondence.

It is generally conceded that the first Committee of Correspondence was formed in Boston in 1764. It wrote legislatures in other colonies to encourage united opposition to both the Sugar and Currency Acts.

Normally, Committees of Correspondence operated primarily within the bounds of a particular colony and were short lived, fading into disuse once the immediate question of the day was disposed of. But this time the flurry of correspondence generated by the Sugar and Currency Acts only grew more widespread in 1765 with the adoption of the Stamp Act.

The House of Commons voted almost offhandedly on the Stamp Act in February, 1765, passing it by a vote of 249 to 49. "Nothing of note in Parliament except one slight day on the American taxes," Horace Walpole was to note.[11] (As quoted, Bowen, p. 262) The Lords also approved the measure without much more debate than it occasioned in the House. Howard quotes the vote a 205-49. The Stamp Act passed Commons on a vote of 205 to 49 and by the House of Lords without "debate, division or protest." [12]

Had Grenville and parliament appreciated the common message in virtually all these petitions, they would have realized that the colonists were opposed in principle to any taxes levied by any body in which they were not represented, period.

There were influential figures in England who applauded the colonists' resistance, including William Pitt and Col. Isaac Barre, a member of the House who seldom agreed with Pitt on anything. It was he who coined a title during the Sugar Act debates that was to be taken up with pride by the colonials—"sons of liberty."

Thanks in part to the resurrection of the committees of correspondence brought about by the Sugar and Currency Acts, a greater sense of community was developing among the colonies. The perceived universal impact of the Stamp Act stimulated the committee outpourings and further solidified a growing "us against them" attitude.

At the behest of the assembly, Connecticut Gov. Thomas Fitch penned "an humble and earnest address" to parliament and the Pennsylvania assembly, putting aside its disagreement about the desirability of becoming a royal colony, agreed to petition against the Stamp Act. Grenville had, according to the address, "instead of a decent demand, sent them a menace, that they should certainly be taxed, and only left them the choice of the manner." [13]

Protests were also heard from North Carolina and Virginia, while the governor of South Carolina dismissed the assembly before it could adopt a similar measure. But it managed to send instructions to its London agent to protest. The Maryland governor managed to keep that colony's assembly from meeting until after the Stamp Act was adopted.

In late 1764, New York appointed a committee of correspondence to petition parliament against both the Sugar Act and the impending Stamp Act.

"It appears plainly," the colony's Robert Livingston wrote, "that these duties are only the beginnings of evil. The stamp duty, they tell us, is deferred, till they see whether the colonies will take the yoke upon themselves, and offer something else as certain. They talk, too, of a land-tax, and to us the ministry appears to have run mad." [14]

Even Rhode Island, with its governor Stephen Hopkins as chairman of its committee of correspondence, sent out a circular letter in which the committee predicted the trade restrictions "must have very fatal consequences" and "will leave nothing to call our own."[15] Foreshadowing what was to come, the letter expressed the hope that some way could be found "for collecting the sentiments of each colony, and for uniting and forming the substance of them into one common defence of the whole."

Loyalists in the colonies as well as Grenville and other members of parliament countered the "no taxation without representation" argument by maintaining that the colonists were "virtually represented" since members of parliament did not represent a particular geographic constituency but rather the empire as a whole.

So up and down the Atlantic seaboard colonists complained about all three revenue measures but, since parliament had a handy rule against receiving petitions against money bills, none were heard. When this was duly reported back to the colonies by their London agents, it increased their frustration as well as their determination.

"The arrogance and blind indifference with which the sentiments and petitions of the colonists were treated during the enactment of this fatal measure," Howard writes, "place the responsibility for the American Revolution squarely on the shoulders of the British government." [16]

Of course, not all historians agree. According to British historian R.J. White, "It cannot be said that the Americans were driven into rebellion by intolerable economic oppression. The rebellion was brought about by an irresistible desire for self-determination on the part of their governing class." [17] But it would have to be a broad "governing class" indeed to encompass George Washington, Thomas Jefferson under the same blanket with Sam Adams and Tom Paine.

American historian John C. Miller agrees with the first half of White's statement.

"Yet it cannot be said that Americans were driven to rebellion by intolerable economic oppression."[18] But, he continues, "The immediate threat to American liberty and well-being after 1765 came not from the restrictions imposed on colonial trade and manufacturing but from parliament's efforts to raise a revenue in the colonies."

In one respect, the Stamp Act might be viewed as the last, and most calamitous, move in what White terms "a conscious policy of asserting British sovereign authority throughout the King's domains."[19] Over the years, many of what had been proprietary or chartered colonies had been converted to royal colonies with royally appointed, rather than elected, governors.

By the end of the Seven Years War, only Pennsylvania and Maryland remained proprietary colonies and Rhode Island and Connecticut as chartered colonies.

In the first few weeks after word was received in the colonies in May that the Stamp Act had been enacted there was a deceptive calm. Governors Hutchinson of Massachusetts, Colden of New York and Sharpe of Maryland all wrote that while there might be some grumbling, all appeared to be well.

"The first organized resistance came from Virginia under the lead of Patrick Henry."[20] On May 29, the Virginia House of Burgesses adopted a motion that it form itself into a committee of the whole to consider what steps should be taken in response to the act.

Henry, who had been a member of the house only nine days at the time, scribbled out seven resolutions which he laid before the house for its consideration. It was during this debate—which was extremely heated—that Henry made his famous comment about Tarquin and Caesar having their Brutus, Charles I his Cromwell and warning that George III "may profit by their example."

While all seven resolves and their preamble were agreed to in committee, the house in formal session was less daring. The last two resolves, along with the preamble, were deleted and the others accepted by narrow margins. The next morning, when Henry was not in attendance, the fifth resolution was also deleted.

Henry's language was blunt to the point of verging on what loyalists would call treason. The resolves stated flatly that the colony was not bound by any law or ordinance that imposed a tax without its consent and that anyone who argued otherwise was "an enemy to his majesty's colony." [21]

Despite the actions of the house to delete portions of the resolves, copies were sent in their entirety—except the third, which was overlooked by mistake—to Philadelphia and New York as having been adopted by the house in Virginia.

Virginia was hard-pressed to get ahead of Massachusetts. On the same day Henry was delivering his resolves, the Massachusetts general court began its session. While the Massachusetts general court took no action as strong as that of the Virginians, it did something that had as much long-term impact—it wrote a letter.

It should be remembered that throughout its early years, Massachusetts was something of an anomaly among the original 13 colonies in that the earliest settlers had brought its charter with them from England, a charter that prescribed its form of government. It was also a fact that "charter rights could not be revoked or modified at the pleasure of the king."[22] Behind this double protection, the Massachusetts settlers felt insulated from some of the influences so prominent in other colonies and so were somewhat bolder in their response than other colonies.

In its June letter, the Massachusetts legislature suggested a meeting of all the colonies to be held in New York the first Tuesday of October to consider the condition to which they would be reduced "by the operation of the acts of parliament for levying duties and taxes."

Response was slow. New Hampshire seemed interested, but named no delegates. New Jersey's assembly in June wrote, wishing them well in their deliberations but declining to participate. Things began to pick up in late summer as word of the Virginia resolves circulated. South Carolina accepted in August and later in the month so did Rhode Island to be followed by Pennsylvania, Connecticut and Maryland. In most of these colonies, resolves along the line of those from Virginia were adopted.

In Virginia, North Carolina and Georgia, the governors refused to convene the assemblies and so they were not represented along with New Hampshire. New Jersey, despite the action of its assembly, was represented by informal delegates.

But as quick as the Virginia and Massachusetts assemblies had been to react to formal notification of the passage of the Stamp Act, they still lagged behind the general reaction. During the months since Grenville served advance notice, merchants, lawyers, tradesmen and a large segment of the general population not only supported the various addresses, petitions and memorials issued by their elected representatives, they took it upon themselves to act.

Under the heading of passive resistance, they banded together in non-importation agreements and encouraged domestic manufacture in defiance of the many and several restrictions imposed by England.

There was also resistance growing of the non-passive sort. Borrowing from Barre, groups blossomed under the "Sons of Liberty" banner in many of the major population centers, particularly in Boston and New York. Initially clandestine groups, they became bolder as they grew in strength, encouraged by an outpouring of pamphlets and newspaper articles opposing not only the Stamp Act itself but parliamentary imposed taxation of any sort.

As they became the focal point of active resistance, the Sons of Liberty soon adopted two primary self-selected objectives—to enforce the non-importation agreements even on merchants who had not signed on voluntarily and to "encourage" by any means available tax stamps agents to resign their posts.

Up until this point, most of the speculation about colonial independence had come either from the English or from foreign observers—principally the French. But with the advent of the Stamp Act, references began to appear from colonial sources.

New Yorker John Morin Scott, writing in the *New York Gazette and Weekly Postboy*, was rash enough to note that "if the welfare of the mother country necessarily requires a sacrifice of the most natural rights of the colonies—their right to make their own laws, and disposing of their own property by representatives of their own choosing—if such is really the case between Great Britain and her colonies, then the connection between them ought to cease; and sooner or later, it must inevitably cease."[23]

The same newspaper in the same month proclaimed the death of "Lady North American Liberty" leaving an only son "prophetically named Independence."

Events in Boston, on the other hand, took a more physical nature. The name of Andrew Oliver, brother-in-law of Chief Justice Hutchinson, had appeared on a published list of tax stamp collectors. Less than a week later, a mob tore down what it believed Oliver intended using as a tax stamp office and used the lumber to burn effigies of him and Lord Bute in Oliver's front yard after first breaking all the windows in the front of his house. Oliver got the message and resigned the following day.

Less than three weeks later, perhaps misunderstanding their sermon of the day before (or perhaps not), a mob ransacked and burned the records in the vice-admiralty court and cleaned out the house of the comptroller of customs. Rev. Jonathan Mahew's text had been "I would they were even cut off which trouble you."

Not ones to let well enough alone, Oliver was compelled in mid-December to swear before a justice of the peace and an assembled throng of about 2,000 that he would not reassume his stamp tax office.

Nor were the residents of Boston alone in their exertions against stamp distributors. By Oct. 31, 1765, the day before the act was to take effect, there wasn't a single distributor left in the 13 colonies. In Newport, R.I., for example, the mob's wrath was turned against Dr. Thomas Moffatt and Martin Howard, along with tax distributor Augustus Johnson. Moffatt and Howard took refuge aboard a British man of war and sailed to England.[24]

"Most stamp masters probably did not suspect when they received their appointments that it was to be a traveling job—usually with a mob at their heels."[25]

While the stamp masters drawn from colonial ranks were

quickly warned away, some appointed in London arrived like sheep to the slaughter.

"Colonel Mercer, the Virginia stamp master, journeyed from London to the Old Dominion to find himself hanging in effigy and even his own father engaged in writing newspaper articles against the Stamp Act." [26]

Nor were the Sons of Liberty above using the Stamp Act riots as a means of evening old scores. Despite the fact that he had opposed the Stamp Act, Chief Justice Thomas Hutchinson's house was ransacked and the manuscript of his history of Massachusetts scattered in the mud.

Even Franklin became an in absentia target of the Philadelphia mob for his counsel to "make as good a night of it as we can."[27] He had procured the stamp master post for his friend and political ally John Hughes. Only the armed intervention of Franklin's partisans kept Hughes from bodily harm.

While rabid resistance grew in the colonies against the Sugar Act, the Currency Act and above all the Stamp Act, all was not well in London.

George Grenville, who managed to kick over the hornet's nest with his colonial measures, also managed to alienate still further his sovereign by failing to secure a measure in Parliament George III wanted.

The Grenville ministry ended in July, 1765, shortly after parliament omitted the king's mother, the Dowager Princess of Wales, from the Regency Bill being drawn at the king's request after his first bout with the serious malady that was to haunt him for the rest of his life. Rather than giving the king the option of naming a regent, the act as passed limited the naming of a regent to the queen "or any other person of the royal family usually residing in Great Britain."

The king was later to agree to the inclusion of "born in England," which effectively barred the German-born princess dowager from being named regent. When he realized that this was a rather public slight on his mother, he asked

Grenville to have the phrase stricken and his mother's name reinserted.

While Grenville declined to seek the change, others in parliament did and the change was made.

Once again, behind the scenes negotiations began to woo Pitt back into government. Word leaked out, however, and when Pitt once again declined the offer, George was left with Grenville. Overly emboldened, Grenville and his cabinet presented a list of demands that verged on the outrageous. Not only did they demand the complete ostracizing of Bute but also his brother, Stuart McKenzie, who had control of patronage in Scotland thanks to Bute's insistence. Also proscribed was George's uncle, the Duke of Cumberland, who had been transformed in Bute's absence from the wicked uncle to George's most trusted advisor.

They also demanded a number of other governmental appointments (and dismissals), all of which the king was forced to grant. On the face of it, Grenville had won a major victory over the king. What he did not understand was how deeply George was offended in having to make the concessions and in that Grenville sealed his political doom.

"From 22 May 1765 to the day of Grenville's death on 13 November, 1770, the king's politics revolved around two aims: first to get Grenville out of office, and next, to make sure he never came back. And he never did." [28]

Through June, negotiations were once again undertaken with Pitt, but with the same negative result. Almost in desperation, George asked his uncle to form a new ministry, which he proceeded to do. Grenville and his supporters, who seemed so much in control in May were out in July after Grenville, as one report states, "was persuaded" to resign.

With Cumberland the head of the new administration in fact if not in title, Charles Watson-Wentworth, the second Marquis of Rockingham, was installed as First Lord of the Treasury and titular head of the administration.

Cumberland and Rockingham had a long history. As a colonel in a volunteer regiment in 1745, he traveled cross country to join Cumberland's forces in their campaign against the Scots. In 1751 he took a seat in the House of Lords and became Lord of the Bedchamber to George II. When George III came to the throne, Rockingham became a victim of Bute's purge of those who supported Pitt after Pitt's resignation in 1762.

As head of the new administration, Rockingham inherited the colonial mess created by Grenville's Sugar, Currency and Stamp Acts.

And so, on Oct. 7, a group of 28[29] delegates from nine colonies convened at New York's City Hall for the Stamp Act Congress, a session that lasted the better part of two weeks. Although they were not officially represented at the congress, there were assurances from both New Hampshire and Georgia that they would support actions.

While some of the delegates wanted to base their grievances on what they saw as violations of their individual charters, Christopher Gadsden of South Carolina successfully argued for a broader, and more basic, common denominator—one that was to provide the philosophical basis that would unite the colonies under a common banner.

"We should stand upon the broad common ground of those natural rights that we all feel and know as man, and as descendants of Englishmen," he wrote. "There ought to be no New England man, no New Yorker, known in the continent, but all of us Americans." [30]

It may have been a hard sell to get past the parochial interests of the individual colonies, but faced with the plain facts of the Sugar, Currency and Stamp Acts and the suspicion that there might be even more to come, it was in the end a telling argument.

The upshot of the congress after weeks of wrangling was a memorial to the House of Lords, a petition to the House of Commons and an address to the king setting out in 13 enumerated points "the grievances under which they labour, by reason of several late Acts of Parliament."

In their resolutions, the colonists insisted they were "entitled to all the inherent rights and liberties of his natural born subjects within the kingdom of Great Britain."

They further built their case step by step: No taxes should be imposed except by their consent, they were not represented in Parliament, the only elected representatives they have are their locally elected legislatures, therefore the legislatures are the only bodies constitutionally able to levy taxes.

Turning to matters legal, the Congress noted that a trial by jury "is the inherent and invaluable right of every British subject in these colonies" and that extension of the power of the Admiralty courts has a "manifest tendency to subvert the rights and liberties of the colonists."

Finally, the resolutions turned to economics. They pointed out to His Majesty that due to the scarcity of specie, "the payment of them absolutely impracticable." The restrictions on colonial trade would render the colonies unable to purchase British goods.

The resolutions conclude by asking the king to seek repeal of the Stamp Act, return the Admiralty Courts to their historic jurisdiction and remove the latest restrictions on colonial trade.

Being adopted less than a month before the Stamp Act was to take effect, the resolutions, petitions and address didn't reach London before the deadline, but it is doubtful they would have made any more impression than the innumerable complaints that had preceded them across the Atlantic.

Chapter 12

In most of the North American colonies, Nov. 1 was greeted with funereal tolling of bells, mock funeral processions and the distribution of handbills cautioning would-be stamp distributors of their possible fate.

The worst disturbance occurred in New York, where the British garrison of some 151 men and officers were confronted in their rather dilapidated fortifications by a mob of some 3,000. While there was no blood shed, the besieged commander, one Colonel James, was obliged to stand by while the mob wrecked his furniture, burned his library and drank up his cellar.[1] The colonel was sufficiently prudent to withhold fire, knowing that that would only prompt an even bigger mob the following day, a mob that would take its vengeance on the garrison.

As a matter of context, it should be noted at this point that the Stamp Act did not apply only to the 13 North American colonies nor did it elicit the same response everywhere it did apply.

"Opposition was most effective in the older, more settled continental colonies; in the newer colonies and in most of the West Indian islands, the act was executed without difficulty."² Canada, East Florida and Georgia pretty well fell into line for differing reasons. The French in Canada had no history of home rule, British military presence was strong in East Florida and in Georgia the governor faced down force with force.

Only the day before the Stamp Act was to take effect, the Duke of Cumberland died in London, removing the glue that had held the Rockingham administration together. Even without his guidance, however, the Rockinghamites displayed rather good sense as word of the commotion rising in the colonies reached London.

Until he was tapped by Cumberland to head the new government, Rockingham's inclinations "had tended more to the turf than politics."³ Possessor of great wealth and holdings, Rockingham's generosity toward his tenants would speak to his humane tendencies.

The fact that Cumberland had nominated Rockingham to head the new government must have been somewhat galling to his nephew the king. Only three years before, Rockingham had resigned as George's Lord of the Bedchamber in protest over Bute's purge of the Pelhamites following Pitt's resignation. In retaliation, George had him removed from all his county offices.

It has been argued that Rockingham's appointment reflects the absence of absolutist tendencies on the part of George. It might also be argued that his acceptance of Rockingham was a measure of his desperation to get rid of Grenville.

In accepting Cumberland's nomination, the 35-year-old Rockingham refused to consider any followers of Grenville—which was fine with the king—or any followers of Bute—which was less acceptable. Rockingham was further handicapped by the fact that Pitt supporters, although courted, like their leader, sat on the sidelines. The death of Cumberland made it all the more desirable that Pitt return to government. Both George and Rockingham agreed on that, but George was not about to attempt another face-to-face meeting with the ex-prime minister. Contacts were therefore carried out through Rockingham and the young Duke of Grafton, then secretary of state and a staunch Pitt supporter.[4]

Pitt, however, in mid-January hedged his conditional acceptance with so many demands that it became apparent he was not about to join the administration as anyone's ally, but as head of the administration with a free hand.

While Rockingham may have had little experience in running the country, according to Edmund Burke's biographer, he had "large experience in the world, he knew the courts and kings of Europe, had dined with Roman cardinals, charmed Italian princesses; he spoke three languages, had managed astutely a large fortune, commanded militiamen in war, ruled the politics of Yorkshire and had been schooled for high public responsibilities by the chiefs of the Whig party."

Despite all that, he and his patchwork administration of old and young Whigs were ill-prepared either by experience or political power for the storm that broke over their doorstep.

The colonial unrest, particularly the non-importation agreements—what might today be called "economic sanctions"—reached during the summer were having a dramatic effect in England, pushing unemployment up and profits for the merchants down. According to one historian, the colonists were indebted to English merchants to the tune of several million pounds sterling and that "they would neither give orders for new goods nor pay for those which they have actually received; and that unless parliament speedily retraced its steps, multitudes of English manufacturers would be reduced to bankruptcy."[5] It was not hard to understand why they added their voices to those of the colonists urging repeal.

As 1765 turned into 1766, parliament discussed and debated for the better part of two months whether to repeal the Stamp Act. During the debates, Grenville demanded to know when the colonies had been emancipated that they might not be taxed, to which Pitt demanded to know in turn when had they been enslaved. Pitt argued that while parliament had the authority to regulate colonial trade, it did not have the right to tax the colonies for revenue without their approval

Pitt's arguments in support of the colonies and for repeal of the Stamp Act led fellow parliamentarian Sir Fletcher Norton to term him "the trumpet to rebellion" and George, at a later date, called him "the trumpet to sedition."

Much of the debate revolved around the distinction between internal and external taxation. Those who opposed repeal saw taxation as part and parcel of England's supremacy over the colonies. Those in favor or repeal, including Pitt, drew a distinction between duties and tariffs laid to regulate colonial trade—which Pitt supported—and taxes laid for the purpose of raising revenue—which he opposed.

Both the debates and the wording of the resolution under parliamentary consideration indicate that both sides finally understood the growing gravity of the situation, both economically and politically.

During the debates, Grenville forecast the disturbances in the colonies growing into revolution if the act was not enforced. Pitt argued that what course parliament took in relation to the Stamp Act would "decide the judgment of posterity on the glory of this kingdom and the wisdom of its government during the present reign."[6]

The resolution under debate states in part that "the continuance of the said act would be attended by many inconveniencies, and may be productive of consequences greatly detrimental to the commercial interests of these kingdoms."

"Inconveniencies" was indeed a quaint word to describe the alternatives to repeal of the act.

On the eve of the vote, Rockingham served notice that his administration would stand or fall on the question.

"If the repeal of the Stamp Act was carried, they would remain in office. If it was defeated, they must resign."[7] (Brooke, p. 129) "Faced with the choice between Rockingham and the repeal of the Stamp Act or Grenville and its enforcement, he preferred Rockingham."[8]

After long and contentious debate, the act was finally repealed on March 18, 1766, by a vote of 275 to 167[9] with the repeal to become effective the following May 1.

Before repeal could gain acceptance, however, parliament had to give notice that it was not caving in to colonial blackmail. To make the point crystal clear, at least in their own minds, and to put the colonists on notice, Parliament prefaced repeal with another act with a title nearly as long as the act itself—An Act for the Better Securing of the Dependency of His Majesty's Dominions in America Upon the Crown and Parliament of Great Britain—otherwise known as The Declaratory Act. The act was adopted in the House of Commons without a division, or recorded vote, and failed unanimity in the House of Lords by only five votes.

With a brevity not displayed in its title, the two-article act stated that several of the colonies had illegally claimed for themselves the "sole and exclusive right of imposing duties and taxes upon His Majesty's subjects." It asserted that Parliament "had, hath, and of right ought to have, full power and authority to make laws and statutes of sufficient force and validity to bind the colonies and people of America, subjects of the crown of Great Britain, in all cases whatsoever."

The second portion of the act declared all colonial resolutions, votes, orders and proceedings that either denied or called that right into question as null and void.

Thanks to the outcry from cities all across England suffering from the colonial boycott, the government had been provided a politically justifiable reason for backing down from the Stamp Act.

"It was essential that parliament did not seem to give way to the riotous colonists; the pleas of the merchants made it possible to regard repeal as a concession to English businessmen in the interest of trade and commerce."[10]

Needless to say, repeal of the Stamp Act was not seen in the same light in the colonies. Depending on one's individual point of view, it was a victory for the Sons of Liberty who intimidated the stamp masters, for the merchants who boycotted English goods or for the loyalists who credited parliament with a display of well-meant generosity.

News of the repeal occasioned fireworks in Boston, an elegant ball in Virginia, much serious drinking in New York and, unfortunately the loss of several lives in Connecticut when the schoolhouse in which they were making fireworks exploded.

Thanks in great part to Grenville, "Americans were remarkably thin-skinned on the subject of British oppression; they cried 'tyranny' upon small provocation and detected black plots against colonial liberty in every act of the British ministry."[11]

"The very fact that George III and his ministers lamented in later years that the colonists had not been forced to obey the Stamp Act reveals how little they understood the basic causes of the dispute that ultimately disrupted the empire."[12]

In the midst of their self-congratulatory celebrations, the colonists tended to disregard the Declaratory Act as an obvious face-saving device not to be considered too seriously. As close as the colonies had been to armed insurrection, surely parliament would not risk further alienating them. Had not England's chief Justice Lord Camden condemned the act in the House of Lords as "Illegal, absolutely illegal, contrary to the fundamental laws of nature, contrary to the fundamental laws of this constitution."[13]

But the act did become a further point of contention for the colonists after they "had time and inclination to discover precisely what had happened."[14]

What the colonists did not reckon on was the repetitive nature of domestic politics in England. By mid-1766, the chasm was once again widening between George and his ministers.

In addition to repealing the Stamp Act, the reformist Rockinghams had succeeded in passing legislation making general warrants—warrants that failed to spell out their specific purpose and scope—illegal and they repealed Grenville's Cider Tax. While these actions displeased the king and his supporters, George countenanced them.

Whether these actions were motivated by a pre-conceived program of reform or whether the existence of a conscious program was created by Burke, Rockingham's one-time private secretary and chief propagandist, in retrospect is a subject of controversy among purists, but the fact remains that they were done.

"In fact, if good intentions and good works are sufficient claims to a nation's confidence, the Rockinghams deserved the confidence more than most. Unfortunately, they lacked almost everything else."[15] Most national administrations on either side of the Atlantic, then as now, would be content to be judged by history on their "good intentions and good works."

Cumberland's death the preceding fall was followed about mid-year with the resignation of Augustus Henry Fitzroy, the third Duke of Grafton, one of two secretaries of state, when he gave up hope that Pitt would ever rejoin the government.

Like Grenville's earlier, but with less reason, the Rockingham administration was obsessed with the possible continuing influence of Bute.

"They began by distrusting the king and they ended by wondering why the king distrusted them."[16]

Somewhat akin to Grenville's earlier power play, the remaining Rockinghamites made the mistake of trying to coerce the king into guaranteeing their continuance in office by trying to hold certain money measures hostage.

On Cumberland's death, a £25,000 allowance became available and George promised that £24,000 would be split among his three younger brothers. The ministers tried to make their retention a condition for their passing the measure through parliament, which was overplaying their hand because it would place the sovereign in the position of breaking his word to his brothers. This was an affront to his personal sense of honor.

Once more the king turned his attentions to wooing the ill Pitt—by now elevated to Lord Chatham—back into government, this time with success. Rockingham was relieved of his office in July and Grafton was installed as secretary of the treasury.

George's decision to once again try to bring Pitt back into government was a vexing one. Grenville was brother to Lord Temple and both were Pitt's brothers-in-law. George hated Grenville and disliked Temple. In previous conversations, Pitt had declined to reenter government unless Temple came with him. If Pitt came back, would that mean readmitting Temple and perhaps even Grenville?

By mid-year, George was convinced through intermediaries that Pitt had indeed split with his brothers-in-law and in July George summoned Pitt to form a new administration. Pitt's acceptance was proof of the old adage about being careful what you wish for, you might get it. It led to what Ayling was the term "The Pitt Fiasco," although in the colonies Pitt's return to government was seen as a tremendous boost for their aspirations. The people of New York even erected a white marble statue of a toga-clad Pitt in Wall Street.[17]

But times had changed since Pitt resigned government five years earlier. Not only had his health deteriorated, but personal animosities had hardened over the years, making his ideal of forming a government irrespective of party essentially impossible.

Not that he didn't try. In his effort to create a broad-based administration, he retained many of the Rockinghams and even went so far as to assure the king that—in reference to Lord Bute—that the king should "not allow ministers to presume to meddle with his private acquaintance."[18]

In the process of forming a new cabinet, however, Rockingham and Newcastle were dismissed. Pitt wanted no former head of government in his cabinet. Grafton was installed as First Lord of the Treasury "an office he tried to avoid and for which he knew himself to be unfit; the brilliant, irresponsible and treacherous Charles Townshend became Chancellor of the Exchequer; and Lord Shelburne, whom the king and nearly everyone else disliked, the other Secretary of State."[19]

"This was not a cabinet for taking decisions; it was cabinet designed to register Pitt's edicts."[20] As Burke was to describe it, the second Pitt administration was "a tessellated pavement without cement," one that was "utterly unsafe to touch and unsure to stand on."

His description was to prove apt. Pitt's failing health and his position in the House of Lords rather than the House of Commons—where he had acquired such fame and control—indeed added up to a rather weak administration despite the presence of three future prime ministers.

Within six months it became weaker still. After the 1766 parliamentary Christmas holiday, Pitt was unable to attend when parliament reconvened in January and in fact did not arrive in London from Bath until early March. Some 10 days later, he had an audience with the king "and forthwith disappeared into seclusion."[21] Although Pitt held his office for another 19 months, "his unwilling deputy, Grafton, was de facto minister."[22]

Today's diagnosis of Pitt's ailment, in addition to his persistent gout, is that he was afflicted with manic depression. He essentially retreated to a single room and refused to see anyone, including the king, Grafton and other members of his administration. Even his meals were passed through a hatch by servants. Numerous letters from George urging him to action generally failed to rouse him.

Like a ship without a rudder, Grafton attempted to maintain some order with the king's assistance, bolstered by a short interview with Pitt in May, 1767. But without Pitt's presence, he faced with the combined opposition of Grenville, the Rockinghams and the Bedfords, otherwise known as the "Bloomsbury Gang," "the members of which were distinguished even in eighteenth century English politics by their rapacity."[23] Grafton was unable to keep order even within his cabinet. "Only their own mutual jealousies prevented the administration's overthrow."[24]

Charles Townshend, chancellor of the exchequer, proved to be the most dangerous loose cannon with his "brilliant fooleries."[25]

Townshend "had decided to go down in history as the man who had settled the affairs of the Empire, East and West."[26] Grafton was unable to prevent Townshend from ushering through parliament in May of 1767 his American Import Duties Bill, as fatal a collection of aggravations for the colonies as parliament had adopted since the Stamp Act itself.

Chapter 13

With the revenue act, Townshend not too subtly endeavored to conceal a revenue bill within a long list of indirect duties on products ranging from paper to lead to glass to tea. These were purportedly intended for the regulation of trade—a function even Pitt and the colonists conceded to parliament—but their real purpose was to raise revenue from the colonies. To make matters even worse, this revenue was to be used to pay the salaries of various colonial officials, thus making them independent of the state legislatures.

With past regulatory measures, if a small surplus was realized, it raised no particular protest. But the Townshend measures were transparent.

Townshend hoped to capitalize on the distinction being drawn by the colonials between an "internal," or direct tax and an "external," or indirect tax. For a time, there were those—including colonial agents in London—who claimed the colonists would not object to an indirect tax if imposed to regulate trade. Grenville, when he headed the administration, derided the distinction. Townshend reasoned that since the duties were collected at the port of entry, they became part of the purchase price to the consumer rather than being added to the purchase as a separate item, they constituted external taxes.

By the time of the Townshend Acts, however, colonials were no longer inclined to make such a fine distinction. By the late 1760s, they were forced to abandon the fiction and recognize a tax was a tax, regardless of the guise. And they were becoming less and less tolerant of any parliamentary taxation.

The opening sentences of the Townshend's Revenue Act were all too clear.

"Whereas it is expedient that a revenue should be raised, in your Majesty's dominions in America, for making a more certain and adequate provision for defraying the charge of the administration of justice, and the support of civil government in such provinces where it shall be found necessary, and towards further defraying the expenses of defending, protecting and securing said dominions . . . ."

A further section of the act provides that the proceeds will be used for the "support of the civil government within all or any of the said colonies or plantations . . ."

Magic words for the colonists: Raising a revenue to pay colonial officials as well as a standing army. And as in earlier acts, it provided for the duties to be paid in hard currency of the realm, something that was in perennial short supply in the colonies.

The act went on to authorize writs of assistance that would allow "the officers of his Majesty's customs to enter and go into any house, warehouse, shop, cellar, or other place . . . to search for and seize prohibited or uncustomed goods."

Other legislation under the general heading of the Townshend Acts created additional Admiralty Courts in Halifax, Boston, Philadelphia and Charleston and established a five-member American Board of Commissioners of the Customs to be seated in Boston. This board was to take the place of the four Surveyor Generals in the colonies, administrators who had little authority to make decisions, but had to refer everything to the Board of Commissioners in London.

In addition to being empowered to make decisions, the board was also empowered to retain all the supporting cast it needed to enforce anti-smuggling laws. Gone were the old customs house workers who were in many cases securely in the pay of the smuggling merchants, and in were a new crop of tide waiters, searchers, collectors, surveyors and clerks.

Less than 10 days after adopting the Revenue Act, parliament passed another motion suspending the New York Assembly until such time as it complied with the Quartering Act of 1765, which required the colony to provide suitable quarters and rations for the royal troops. The colony was the military headquarters for British troops in North America, and supplying housing and provisions for a large number of soldiers posed a rather heavy burden on the colony. Following the lead of Blackstone, the leading legal authority of the era, New Yorkers saw the Mutiny Act as a tax on the citizens and, as such, the assembly declined to provide for the troops, bringing about the suspension until such time as the colony complied.

In the suspension of the New York assembly and the passage of the Revenue Act, Miller contends, Townshend was displaying his inconsistency. Punishing the New York assembly while other colonial assemblies were equally in defiance of the Mutiny Act was intended to send a message to the other colonies without offending them all, which might tend to drive the colonies closer together. Yet in the Revenue Act he did exactly that. He failed to learn from Grenville's earlier Stamp Act experiment.

While other colonies weren't as openly defiant as New York, most found ways to make compliance with the Mutiny Act appear as voluntary contributions rather than being made under duress. New York, meanwhile, unsure of their support from other colonies, voted by a single vote to supply the troops shortly before the October, 1767, deadline. Like the other colonies, however, they made their £1,500 appropriation appear as a voluntary gift.

In England, enforcement of the Mutiny Act became a matter of principle. The colonies must be made to comply with parliamentary edicts or the foundation of the empire would be threatened. These concerns helped bring Grenville, the Duke of Bedford, Townshend and other hardliners back into power, a shift in parliamentary policy that the essentially leaderless Chatham administration was powerless to stop.

Once again, domestic politics in England shaped policies affecting the North American colonies—the land taxes and the East India Company.

When "Champagne Charlie" Townshend claimed before parliament that he knew how to extract a revenue from the colonies, and thus reduce the land tax in England, the prospect was irresistible.

As for the East India Company, thanks to its government-granted monopoly it had been plundering the riches of India for years to the individual enrichment of its officials and shareholders, but the country was gaining little in the way of revenue. By the middle of the 1760s its revenues were decreasing but any effort to divest the company of its quasi-governmental status was naturally opposed by those who were benefiting, led in parliament by Townshend.

The East India Company was left in possession of its revenues and profits on the promise of paying £400,000 a year, an obligation that was to figure in later events.

Stymied in that direction, the lure of revenue from the colonies was all the more attractive.

The events that sprang from Townshend's brain storm also proved irresistible.

As far as the Customs Commission was concerned, it was not by coincidence that it was to be settled in Boston.

"Boston, to conservatives everywhere in the empire, was a horrible example of the rule of numbers; the dire results of giving the common people an equal voice with gentlemen of property and breeding in the management of public affairs seemed exemplified in this mobbish metropolis."[1]

Perhaps fortunately for him, the unpredictable Townshend died unpredictably not long after his measures were adopted, thereby sparing him the turmoil that was to come. From the adoption of Townshend's Revenue Act, relations between the colonies and the mother country spiraled downward at an ever-increasing rate.

By 1768 Pitt, aware that the administration of which he was supposed to be leader was adopting policies he disapproved of—like the Townshend duties—and that many of his supporters were being dismissed from government, resigned, an action the king took to be desertion.

Before he did, however, he was approached by George and Grafton on the question of an alliance to strengthen the faltering administration. To George, it was a choice between the Rockinghams and the Bedfords, neither of whom the king relished bringing back into government. Pitt "listlessly made it plain that he preferred the Bedfords—as the lesser of two evils."[2]

Grafton, more through a sense of duty than desire, remained as prime minister in name as well as function for another two years. But he was not in command of the cabinet as the Bedfords returned to positions of influence. A third Secretaryship of State was created out of the Southern Department to deal specifically with the American colonies, removing the colonial administration from Lord Shelburne and delivering it to Irish born Wills Hill, Lord Hillsborough, who was also head of the Board of Trade.

George III was to say he did not know "a man of less judgment than Lord Hillsborough."[3] while Benjamin Franklin biographer Jared Sparks termed him "a man of integrity and honest purposes but too fond of his own opinions and obstinate in carrying out his schemes." His lack of judgment and conviction of his opinions were to bode ill for the colonies.

Initially, colonial reaction to the Townshend duties was about the same as it had been to the Stamp Act—constitutional petitions, boycotts and physical intimidation of those charged with enforcing the new duties. By now, the colonials were openly rejecting all efforts at parliamentary taxation, whether internal or external.

It is one of the most delicious ironies of history that the very arguments being employed by the colonists against parliament were the same ones espoused in England nearly 80 years earlier to justify the Glorious Revolution that overthrew the absolutist monarchy of James II in 1688-89.

In 1690, John Locke penned *Two Treatises of Government* in which he made the case that there were certain principles of what he termed "natural law" governing what was right and wrong. Among other things, he held that a legislature was supreme over the crown since it supposedly represented the people. While he had parliament in mind, the colonials substituted their legislatures, where they were represented, in place of parliament, where they were not.

Locke's contention that taxes could not be levied without consent of parliament the colonists interpreted as consent of the colonial legislatures.

"His conviction that subjects might rebel if their government ceased to respect the law—which clearly referred to the tyranny of James II—was used by Americans to sanction rebellion against the king and parliament."[4]

Perhaps dearest to the hearts of the colonials was Locke's stand on the unilateral seizure of property.

"If any one shall claim a power to lay and levy taxes on the people by his own authority and without such consent of the people, he thereby invades the fundamental law of property and subverts the end of government."[5]

Unwittingly, one of England's premier political philosophers provided the ammunition that eventually blew holes in the British Empire. What can justify one revolution can also justify another.

It was his arguments that were to be heard more and more frequently blowing eastward across the Atlantic, words that had once served their purpose on the island but with their original purpose accomplished, no longer rang as true in the mercantilist undertaking that the empire had become. Locke's dissertation was "a museum piece, not a manifesto calling the oppressed to arms."[6]

But Locke's appeal to "natural law" received particularly strong support from the colonial pulpits of the day, especially in New England.

"No people are under a religious obligation to be slaves if they are able to set themselves at liberty," Jonathan Mayhew wrote Thomas Hollis, the benefactor of Harvard, in 1765.[7]

The influence of the clergy can be seen in the sacking of Hutchinson's Boston home after hearing a sermon during the Stamp Act crisis. The clergy's influence had not diminished in the interval.

In February, 1768, Samuel Adams, as clerk of the Boston town meeting, penned on behalf of the Massachusetts assembly a circular letter that was dispatched to all other colonial legislatures that really raised the royal hackles.

In the letter, Adams argues that parliament, while "the supreme legislative power over the whole empire," has its bounds in the English constitution. He further argues that the North American colonists "who acknowledge themselves bound by the ties of allegiance, have an equitable claim to the full enjoyment of the fundamental rules of the British constitution."

All of which is followed by a very large "but."

Adams and the Massachusetts legislature argued that the British constitution also contained "a fundamental law and ever held sacred and irrevocable." That law, according to the circular letter, was that "what a man has honestly acquired is absolutely his own, which he may freely give but cannot be taken from him without his consent."

Therefore, the letter continues, the parliamentary acts "are infringements of their natural and constitutional rights because as they are not represented in the British parliament" and therefore their property is being granted without their consent.

The circular letter also took shots at royal payment of governors, judges and other civil officials as creating "a tendency to subvert the principles of equity and endanger the happiness and security of the subject." Also mentioned in passing were the quartering act and the customs commission as further instances of actions that were, at least in Massachusetts' view, becoming "dangerous to the liberty of the people."

The letter concluded by inviting input from the other colonies.

Needless to say, a copy of the letter was forwarded to London as soon as it appeared and in April Lord Hillsborough, the new Secretary of State for the Colonies, issued an order to the royal governors. In it, all the conciliatory phrases discussed in cabinet were removed. Rather, he called on them to take every measure possible to prevent the letter being considered by their assemblies but to treat it "with the contempt it deserves."

"But if notwithstanding these expectations and your earnest endeavors, there should appear in the assembly of your province a disposition to receive or give any countenance to this seditious paper, it will be your duty to prevent any proceeding upon it by an immediate prorogation or dissolution."

Which is what happened in several colonies.

"Lord Hillsborough's Circular Letter deserved to rank not far below the Stamp Act and Townshend duties among the contributions of British ministers to the formation of the American Union."[8]

Acting on Hillsborough's demand, Massachusetts governor Bernard put the matter before the Massachusetts assembly in June. After nine days of debate, the assembly refused to rescind an action of a preceding assembly. Gov. Bernard responded by shutting down the assembly.

Angered by Hillsborough's letter, reaction in other colonies was similar. The Georgia House of Commons not only elected to hear the Massachusetts circular letter that spring, it determined that it was a proper exercise of the right to petition the throne, whereupon Gov. James Wright dissolved the assembly.

Even Pennsylvania, which up until that time had been the most compliant of all, was stirred into approval of the Massachusetts letter. New Hampshire, Connecticut and New Jersey also went on record as approving the Massachusetts letter.

Within days of the dissolution of the Massachusetts General Assembly, Boston merchants signed a non-importation agreement similar to the one adopted during the Stamp Act confrontation. Merchants in New York also adopted their version about the same time.

Even before the Massachusetts assembly declined Gov. Bernard's demand it rescind the circular letter, Gen. Thomas Gage—the British military commander in America—was ordered in June to send troops to Boston to occupy Castle William and the admiralty was ordered to station several armed vessels in Boston harbor.

The harbor was already occupied by the 50-gun *Romney* and the captain had taken to impressing Americans for his crew, a circumstance that had caused a number of hostile encounters between the sailors and civilians.

One the same day that a group rescued a resident from the grasp of a press gang, John Hancock's sloop *Liberty* arrived in port laden with Madeira wine. "Attempting to inspect the cargo, the collector was seized by the crew and locked on board while contraband goods were landed and a false entry made at the custom house."[9] This resulted in the ship being seized and anchored close under the *Romney's* guns.

As might have been anticipated, this brought out the mob with resulting damage to the homes of the controller and customs inspector. The customs officers took refuge on the *Romney* and, later, at Castle William. The incident also brought a resolution from the assembly asking Bernard to order the removal of the *Romney,* but the governor declared that was beyond his jurisdiction.

Not that Boston was alone in resorting to physical force against customs officials. Reaction in Rhode Island was particularly physical. At Providence, Jesse Saville, a customs officer's assistant, was treated to a protective coating of tar and feathers and another, Charles Dudley, was beaten up by a gang, none of whom were ever identified; in Newport, a citizen was killed in an argument with a royal midshipman and later a moored revenue cutter was burned.

These incidents prompted a Boston town meeting in mid-September at which a series of resolutions were voted once again calling into question the legality and constitutionality of taxation without representation and of maintaining a standing army among the people during peacetime.

Citing legislation adopted during the reign of William and Mary following the Glorious Revolution nearly a century before, Boston residents maintained that under acts passed by parliament taxing of the people except as provided for by the colony's General Assembly was in violation of the colony's royal charter and "in violation of the undoubted natural rights of subjects."

Also citing legislation of the same period, the resolutions stated "the raising or keeping a standing army within the kingdom in time of peace, unless it be with the consent of parliament, is against the law." Such an army, the resolutions continued, "would be an infringement of their natural, constitutional and charter rights" and using such an army to enforce laws made without the consent of the people would be a "grievance."

The resolutions, in Franklin's words, created "a prodigious clamour"[10] when they were received in London.

On the very day that the convention ended its six-day deliberations, two regiments of the line, complete with artillery arrived in the town from Halifax and by four in the afternoon were parading on Boston Common.

In December, both the House of Commons and House of Lords endorsed a resolution censuring the Massachusetts assembly for not rescinding its circular letter and expressing satisfaction in the way the situation was being handled in Boston. Parliament went even further. It recommended the resurrection of a statute passed under Henry VIII in the 1500s whereby anyone accused of treason outside the kingdom might be brought to England for trial.

The insertion of troops into such a fractious town as Boston, already the site of the Board of Customs Commissioners, was really asking for trouble.

Meanwhile, back in England, the John Wilkes fiasco was playing itself out again. Wilkes, author and publisher of *The North Briton,* returned to England in 1768 from five years of voluntary exile in France after being found guilty of seditious and obscene libel. Not only did he return, he managed to get himself elected to Parliament from Middlesex.

Although Wilkes' outlawry was dismissed on a technicality, Grafton could not simply overlook his past transgressions. Wilkes was still sentenced to two years in prison plus a hefty fine. Thanks to the largesse of his supporters, he was not lacking for the finer things in life even in prison.

When he was unable to appear in parliament when it convened in May, a mob threatened to storm the prison and escort him to the House of Commons, precipitating a riot in which some half-dozen people were killed.

Grafton undertook to have Wilkes barred from his seat in the house and despite parliamentary action in February, 1769, to set aside his election, voters in Middlesex reelected him two weeks later without opposition The next day, he was once again expelled from the House. Followed by another election and another expulsion.

Finally, in desperation, the house seated a defeated rival, Henry Lawes Luttrell, even though he had received only a scant number of votes, on the basis of a parliamentary resolution that Wilkes was unfit to sit in the House. This high-handed negation of the vote of the people was widely seen as a constitutional violation and the resulting uproar further contributed to the collapse of the Grafton administration. It wasn't until 1774, and under a new administration, that parliament allowed Wilkes to take his seat and "the record of the House's folly expunged from its journals."[11]

Barred from the House, Wilkes stood for and was elected a magistrate for the City of London, where he proved to be a continuing thorn in the side of parliament. At one point, he had printers brought before him on the charge that they published parliamentary debates, a prohibited practice. He not only dismissed the charges, he encouraged them to do it again. During the ensuing argument between parliament and the city government, Lord Mayor Brass Crosby was arrested. Although parliament never rescinded its prohibition, neither did it try to enforce it.

All in all, the Grafton administration succumbed to an accumulation of domestic as well as international events, but primarily domestic. Without Pitt, Grafton could not control the cabinet or the House and, with the return of the Bedfords, his control was even less.

Not only had he to cope with Wilkes and the letters of "Junius"—a Wilkes supporter who held the administration up to unremitting public ridicule—Ireland was creating problems again. Possible warfare with Spain and France was once again on the horizon. Grafton even had problems moving the annual budget through the House. And then there was his divorce.

Perhaps the final blow was when Pitt recovered enough in the summer of 1769 to see the direction the administration was moving and to attack it.

In January, 1770, just two weeks into the new session of parliament, Grafton threw in the sponge and resigned, an action George once again termed "desertion." Within a week, three cabinet ministers had resigned—Grafton having been preceded by Lord Camden, the Lord Chancellor, and the Marquess of Granby, the commander-in-chief.

Grafton was succeeded by a cousin, Frederick Lord North, a member of parliament for 16 years and a veteran of the Newcastle and Bute administrations, but who had resigned when Rockingham came to power. He reenlisted in the Pitt ministry as joint Paymaster of the Forces and later as a privy counselor. On Townshend's untimely death, North advanced to Chancellor of the Exchequer and in 1768 to Leader of the House of Commons under Grafton. "North got to the top just by being around and in default of anyone better."[12]

In North, George apparently he felt he had found someone with whom he could communicate as he had with Bute. His father has been Prince George's governor and they had even acted together in a juvenile production at Leicester House, Prince Frederick's residence.

"North came close to being the ideal democratic statesman. He never said anything that could not be readily understood; he never appeared cleverer than the average man; and he was acutely sensitive to public opinion."[13]

But, states White, "Politically considered, the years of Lord North's administration are bad, sad years, years of broken empire, defeat in arms, a melancholy struggle to survive."[14]

Chapter 14

The year before acceding to the post of prime minister, North, according to Alexander Boswell, the preeminent biographer of the day, "had long . . . indulged most unfavorable sentiments of our fellow subjects in America . . . a race of convicts who ought to be thankful for anything we allow them short of hanging."[1]

On the other hand, Brooke states "In Lord North, the king found an efficient Leader of the House of Commons"[2] while Hibbert notes that North "certainly proved himself to be an astute manager and manipulator of the House of Commons."[3]

Efficient and astute though he may have been in controlling the House of Commons and in carrying out George's political agenda, he nevertheless has the dubious distinction of presiding over the loss of the North American colonies.

Among his other political attributes, North was one to take a close sniff at which way the political winds were blowing.

George offered North the Treasury post after Grafton's resignation, but North deferred his answer until late in

January. He was waiting to determine whether parliament would approve a resolution censuring the administration for its seating Luttrell in the Middlesex elections over Wilkes.

Once that vote proved favorable to the government, he accepted the position, one that he was to retain for 12 years.

"During the next three years," Howard maintains, "colonial affairs were directed mainly by royal orders."[4]

North inherited a whirlwind larger and more serious than any of his predecessors. Colonial affairs were degenerating from confrontations between legislatures and governors, between the Sons of Liberty and the tax collectors, to face-to-face encounters between the public and the British troops brought in to enforce the Townshend duties.

As usual, Boston was the worst trouble spot. It was, after all, the largest of North America's four population centers, followed by New York, Philadelphia and Charleston. While there were disturbances in New York, they were much less frequent or intense in either Philadelphia of Charleston.

In January, 1770, for example, the New York Sons of Liberty took exception to the state legislature granting £1,500 in mid-December for supplies for the British troops, even though the assembly was facing dismissal and the grant was framed as a voluntary gift. This led to a clash of about 40 Sons of Liberty and a like number of British troops in what came to be called the Battle of Golden Hill. Injuries were numerous, but there were no fatalities.

Boston being founded by the most distinctly dissident of early settlers, it is not surprising that it was the leading political stage of the day. Such a leader, in fact, that the history of the time essentially reads like a history of Boston. But the other colonies were watching the events in Boston closely.

Late in 1769, the first really serious encounter between the mob and soldiers was narrowly averted when two Bostonians judged not to be in sympathy with the ongoing boycott of English goods were chased through King Street and kept at bay only at gun point. The two took refuge in the British guardhouse. Despite appeals to Lt. Gov. Hutchinson, no protection was offered and the main culprit finally escaped the guardhouse and sailed for England, where he presented his grievances to Lord Hillsborough. Hutchinson was well aware of the likely consequences if he called out the troops. The city was effectively in the hands of the assembly, the hardliners and their supporting cast, the mob.

But the near miss only forestalled the inevitable. Throughout the winter, intimidation and even physical assaults continued against any merchants who failed to abide by the current non-importation agreement. But basically, the disturbances were between conflicting colonists. But even those turned deadly in February when Tory merchant Ebenezer Richardson fatally wounded 11-year-old Christopher Seider (or perhaps Snider) who was among a multitude of other boys busily smashing Richardson's windows. Orchestrated by Sam Adams, young Seider's funeral was "the largest perhaps ever known in America."[5]

Boston was in foment and the presence of troops—admittedly powerless against the multitudes—only aggravated the situation. Most of the civilian justices of the peace were in league with the colonials and the rest were in fear of their lives if they went against the mob. Despite repeated entreaties from Lt. Gov. Hutchinson for them to do their duty, the town was clearly not under control of the government, and both the government and the citizens knew it.

"By now, as February 1770 turned into March, the fallacy of sending the soldiers had become clear to the loyalists, the radicals and, most important, even to the military."[6]

The British trooper was not exactly well paid and many of the 600 stationed in Boston sought employment in the civilian sector to augment their meager salaries. On March 2, a soldier looking for work was insulted by a ropewalk worker that if the soldier wanted a job he could come and clean out the man's outhouse, or words to that effect. The ensuing fist fight sparked something of a small riot.

Only three days later occurred one of the landmark events in pre-Revolutionary history—the Boston Massacre. Accounts of the incident vary, but the bare facts seem to be that an early evening crowd of youngsters started taunting a British sentry at the same King Street guardhouse. By about 9 p.m. a squad was sent to the sentry's assistance while the crowd, attracted by the ringing church bells that usually signified a fire, had swelled to some 300 to 400. The detail, under the command of Capt. Thomas Preston, arrayed itself facing the crowd, which continued to press as close as the bayonets would permit. Even when the soldiers loaded their muskets, the crowd persisted in haranguing the troops.

The soldiers were pressed so tight that the soldiers had to use bayonets to keep the crowd at bay, but they were close enough to hit the muskets with their clubs.

Unfortunately, the mob was laboring under the misapprehension that the soldiers could not fire without the authorization of a civil authority and none were present. What they did not take into account was that the soldiers were free to protect their lives.

Exactly what happened next depends on whose account is heard. There was a division of opinion as to whether Preston said "Fire" or "Don't fire." The nature of the actual firing—first one musket and then another in random fashion—would tend to support the second contention.

Whatever the case, once the smoke had cleared and the soldiers withdrew to their barracks, five men had been killed—four on the spot and the fifth four days later. (or perhaps three on the spot and two died later; again, accounts differ) In addition, six others were wounded.

The incident caused a variety of meetings and hearings of the city fathers that lasted until about 3 a.m. Capt. Preston gave himself up for arrest and he and the other members of the detail were later tried.

"It may be true that immediately the townsmen were far more guilty than the soldiers. The real responsibility rests upon the statesmen who created the conditions rendering such a result almost inevitable."[7]

While it has also been suggested that the entire confrontation was set up and egged on by the radical leadership, there is no credible evidence that even the most avid leader would deliberately seek bloodshed for political reasons.

On the other hand, the radicals wasted little time in making the best of a propaganda bonanza. A multitude of "eye witness" accounts appeared in the newspapers of the day and Paul Revere's moving, although historically inaccurate, engraving of the shooting was on the streets in color within a few days. Word of the incident was also broadcast throughout the other colonies.

There are two ironies connected with the Boston Massacre. One is the date. On the very day the shooting took place, parliament voted to repeal all of the Townshend duties with the exception of the tax on tea, which was retained by a majority of one.[8]

The second irony came in October, when Preston finally went on trial. Chief among his defense attorneys was none other than John Adams. Adams also defended the soldiers in their trial shortly after. The acquittal of all but two of the defendants indicated that not all Bostonians were consumed by the passions of the moment, but that law still had its place in the overall scheme of things. Two troopers were convicted of manslaughter, but escaped with branding.

However, the troops were prudently removed to Castle William in Boston harbor to minimize the possibility of a repeat occurrence. Before spring was over, they were joined by most members of the customs commission and their families.

In writing to Gen. Gage in New York after the shooting, Hutchinson conceded "government is at an end and in the hands of the people."[9]

Meanwhile, the new prime minister in England was trying to find the best way out of the mess he inherited from Grafton.

His first step was to consider repeal of the Townshend duties.

The fact that London merchants, smarting under the colonial non-importation agreements, were among those calling for their repeal provided North and his supporters with the political cover needed. Exports to America had fallen from £2,378,000 in 1768 to £1,634,000 the following year.[10] Not only were the merchants losing current sales to North America, they were facing the prospect that their American debtors would be unable to pay for past purchases. While in 1700 the colonies consumed only about 10 percent of British exports, by 1772 that figure had jumped to better than one-third.[11] Extension of credit to the colonies was proving a double-edged sword for the London merchant.

"I heartily wished to repeal the whole of the law . . . if there had been a possibility of repealing it without giving up that just right which I shall ever wish the mother country to possess, the right of taxing the Americans."[12]

Parliament, in its debate over repealing the Townshend acts, elected to retain the tea tax for the symbolic one alluded to by North.

"The retention of the tax on tea was due largely to the personal influence of the king; and that he was able to have his way in so useless and so perilous a measure reveals the utter ineptitude of British statesmanship in this critical period."[13]

"By the 1730s, close to a million pounds of tea a year were being imported from China to Britain by the East India Company, which could sell it on the London market for four times what it had paid in China."[14]

In one respect it was a win-win situation. Parliament preserved its fiction of taxing the Americans and the Americans simply went on smuggling Dutch tea. The

Americans also relaxed their embargo on those goods on which the taxes had been removed.

Trade with the colonies rebounded with the end of the embargo, rising to £4,200,000 in 1771.[15]

After the emotional reactions that followed the deaths of Christopher Seider and the victims of the "Boston massacre," the colonial atmosphere relapsed into a pattern of continuing confrontations between the colonials on the one hand and the tax collectors and customs agents on the other.

While things improved on the trade front, at least as far as the English merchants were concerned, there was a string of constant irritations for the colonists, especially in Massachusetts. Many of these sprung from the royal proclivity for issuing orders to his governors that had the effect of law, thus usurping parliament. Parliamentary objections, however, were effectively stifled by his efficient manager of the House of Commons, Lord North.

In Massachusetts, for example, Lt. Gov. Hutchinson, on orders from London, decreed in 1770 that the general court would meet March 15 in Cambridge rather than Boston. Members of the house asked to see the instructions, but Hutchinson refused, purportedly again on specific royal instructions. Hutchinson, again on royal orders, removed the colonial troops from Castle William and turned it over to British regulars, which the colonials took as an indication of a lack of royal confidence and royal displeasure.

In 1771, he announced his appointment as governor succeeding Bernard and in July he vetoed the annual income tax bill that paid the salaries of the crown officers. In June, 1772, he further announced that henceforth his salary would be paid by the crown and in August "came the news that in the same way the judges were to be made dependent on the royal favor."[16]

Naturally, these actions were seen as assaults on the colony's charter and were resisted them because they insulated the governor and judges from the general court's control of the purse strings, which was the only control it had over the crown offices.

Nor was all calm elsewhere during the early 1770s.

In Rhode Island, where the economy of the tiny colony relied on trade, legal and illegal, the expanse of Narragansett Bay, with its many solitary inlets and coves, proved difficult for the British customs patrol to watch. But they tried, much to the annoyance of the smuggling trade. In 1769, while the crew was ashore, the customs ship coincidentally named *Liberty* was boarded, cut adrift, its mast cut down and then the ship was scuttled and its boats burned.

Not that the Rhode Islanders didn't believe they had just cause to take their revenge on the British ships. Not only did they occasionally seize perfectly legal ships and cargoes, they were not above impressing seamen from American ships when they were shorthanded.

His majesty's sloop *Gaspee,* which had been on patrol in the Pennsylvania area since 1764, was particularly hated for the large number of seizures it had affected. After a refitting, the ship was reassigned to the New England coast to allow tempers in the Mid-Atlantic colonies to cool off.

But its new captain, Lt. William Dudington, found no more hospitable welcome than he had received further south. In addition to impressing seamen and harassing innocent coastal shippers, he was prone to commandeer livestock and other provisions from area farmers without permission or payment.

The offended Rhode Islanders exacted their revenge in early June, 1772, when the *Gaspee* was lured into shallow water and ran aground while chasing the *Hannah.* When word reached Providence in the early evening, it wasn't long before some 65 volunteers were rounded up and headed for the stranded vessel. The crew was overpowered and put off in boats, along with Lt. Dudington, who was wounded in the fray. The raiders then rowed back to the ship and burned it to the waterline.

"But from June 10, 1772, until a year later, when the investigation of the *Gaspee* incident was closed, not one person in Providence admitted to knowing about it in advance, or knowing either before or after the fact, the name of any person involved."[17]

Further south, the colonial government of North Carolina was having its own troubles. Although it was of a different sort than that of Boston or New York, it nevertheless brought about armed conflict.

Settlers in the western region of the state, fed up with the corrupt officials in their midst and the lack of law and order from the administration of Gov. William Tyron, decided to take the law into their own hands and in 1768 organized what they called the Regulators.

For some two years the Regulators held sway in the back country, but the established government obviously could not countenance the situation forever. After several incidents, Tyron called out the militia in 1771 and marched to the west. In a pitched battle at Alamance in May, the Regulators were defeated and several of the leaders arrested and hanged for rebellion. Hundreds took an oath of allegiance, but thousands more fled further west across the mountains into what in now Tennessee.

"The battle of Alamance was not the first battle of the Revolution, as it has often been called, but a chapter in the story of the internal sectional conflict."[18]

Incidents like the Boston massacre, the Regulator uprising and the burning of the *Gaspee* naturally hardened the resolution in England that the colonies must be brought to heel in light of the Declaratory Act. But once again, domestic politics shaped parliamentary actions. With the East India Company verging on bankruptcy, partially from mismanagement and partially from the colonial embargo, parliament in April, 1773, passed two measures—the Regulating Act for India and the Tea Act. The first essentially brought the company under the control of parliament rather than the East India Company while the second gave the company a monopoly on the tea trade to North America.

Through a combination of mismanagement, the siphoning off of vast sums of money, competition from the Dutch and others, along with its £400,000 a year commitment to the government, the company was virtually bankrupt.

To assist the company, parliament allowed the company to import its tea directly into the colonies. This, parliament reasoned, would increase the company's profits by cutting out the middle man and at the same time underprice the smuggled Dutch tea.

Despite warnings against shipping taxed tea into the colonies, the *Dartmouth* arrived in Boston in November to be followed by the *Beaver* and the *Eleanor* with a total of some 342 casks of tea valued at £10,000. The cargo remained aboard for more than two weeks while efforts were made to arrange the landing of the shipment. On the night of Dec. 16, after a mass meeting, about 40 colonials, thinly disguised as Indians, divided into three parties, boarded the ships and dumped the entire shipment into the harbor.

"The Boston Tea Party brought matters to a head. Here was a defiance of authority which the British government could not afford to ignore. Here was an act of rebellion which the Americans could not afford to disclaim."[19]

"When the news reached London (at the end of January, 1774) the cry went up for coercion and the reactionaries in the British government became supreme."[20]

"When the Boston Tea Party turned the world upside down the king agreed with North that stern action must be taken."[21]

In early February, George met with Gen. Gage, who was on leave from his post as commander-in-chief in North America. Gage was of the opinion that a show of force would force the colonists to back down. In July, that opinion was reinforced by Thomas Hutchinson, late governor of Massachusetts.

There were those in parliament who saw the situation as something more than an insoluble standoff between two fixed and irreconcilable positions. During the parliamentary debates over repeal of the tea tax in April, Charles James Fox declared that "Countries should always be governed by the will of the governed."[22] But the idea was foreign to the British. Like the ideas of John Locke adopted by the Americans earlier, the administration saw nothing but chaos if carried to the extreme. No one wanted to see Ireland governed by the Irish or India by the Indians.

And so was enacted between March and June, 1774, a quartet of punitive laws directed against Massachusetts that proved to be the proverbial bale of hay that broke the camel's back.

Chapter 15

Collectively, they were called the "Coercive Acts" in Britain, but in the colonies they became the "Intolerable Acts." Thanks to the level of anger generated in England by the Boston Tea Party, the coercive acts of 1774 aroused little opposition in the House of Commons.

On the last day of March, parliament adopted the Boston Port Act, closing the harbor to all shipping but coasters carrying fuel and supplies "for the necessary use and sustenance of the inhabitants of the said town of Boston." The act, which also transferred the seat of government to Salem and made Marblehead the customs port of entry, "raced through parliament with few voices raised against it."[1] Both Gen. Gage, who had served in America, and ex-Massachusetts Gov. Hutchinson assured George that the Americans would wilt in the face of resolute action on the part of the British. Such was the quality of advice he was receiving from his "experts."

The closure was to remain until three conditions were met: That the East India Company was compensated £9,000 to £10,000 for the 342 chests of jettisoned tea, that the injured customs officers were compensated for their injuries and until George was convinced peace was sufficiently restored.

To close the port of a town that relied on the sea for its very commercial existence was of course calamitous. Had they been sufficiently aware, Gage and the other British officials in Boston might have taken the amount of provisions that flowed into the city not only from outlying towns but from neighboring colonies as well as an indication that coercion might not produce the contrition they expected.

The Boston Port Act was followed in May by the Massachusetts Government Act and the Administration of Justice Act, both adopted the same day.

The Administration of Justice Act noted that the colony's elected officials "hath, for some time past, been such as had the most manifest tendency to obstruct, and in great measure, defeat the execution of the laws; to weaken the attachment of his majesty's well-disposed subjects in the said province to his majesty's government, and to encourage the ill-disposed among them to proceed even to acts of direct resistance to, and defiance of, his majesty's authority."

Therefore, the act proceeded to disband the elected assembly which had passed "many dangerous and unwarrantable resolves" to be replaced by one appointed by the governor. The governor was also given power to appoint and dismiss all law officers. Both members of the appointed assembly and the law officers were to serve at the will and pleasure of the governor. There were to be no town meetings without prior written approval of the government and juries of all levels, rather than being elected, were to be selected by the sheriff.

The Administration of Justice Act (known locally as The Murder Act) provided that the governor might, at his discretion, remove any trial "for murder or other capital offense" from Massachusetts to another colony or even to England. The justification given in the act is to remove any apprehension on the part of magistrates or "any of his majesty's subjects aiding and assisting them" that they might be brought to trial "before persons who do not acknowledge the validity of the laws."

Finally, in early June, parliament upgraded the Quartering Act of 1765. Originally, the act called upon the colonists to provide shelter and necessities for the troops and the use of unoccupied buildings. With the arrival of additional troops in Boston, accommodations at Castle William were inadequate. The act was therefore amended to allow for the forced billeting of troops in inns and even private, occupied homes.

These acts were opposed by both the Rockingham and Chatham factions, "but passed easily enough." [2]

"Justified or unjustified, wise or unwise, they were strongly backed by such British public opinion as took any interest."[3]

To these four punitive acts was added, at mid-June, the Quebec Act which extended to boundaries of that province south and west, thereby hemming in the northeast colonies from any westward expansion and, in effect, making those inhabitants in the Ohio Valley Canadians. It also reaffirmed recognition of the Canadians' Catholic religion, a recognition that was part of the Peace of Paris in 1763.

Although the reasons behind the act had little to do with the colonies, they saw it as yet another transgression by parliament by violating their "sea-to-sea" charters, by cutting off various commercial companies that hoped to settle the Ohio Valley and beyond and, especially among the New England Puritans, promotion of Catholicism.

One other action taken by George at this time was naming Gage, already commander-in-chief of the British forces in North America, as Massachusetts governor to succeed Hutchinson. Hutchinson's departure for England on June 1, 1774, was precipitated to a great extent by the complete disdain with which he was held by the residents of the colony.

A little espionage on the part of Ben Franklin, in London in 1772 as agent for Massachusetts and other colonies, played a large part in reducing Hutchinson to impotence.

Franklin came into possession (no one knows from whom) of letters written by Hutchinson as governor in 1768 and 1769, Chief Justice Oliver and Charles Paxton, a member of the tax commission, to Thomas Whatley, a former member of parliament and a former secretary of the treasury under Grenville.

In one of his letters, Hutchinson expressed the opinion that "there must be an abridgement of what are called English liberties" if the colony was to be controlled for he was dubious "whether it is possible to project a system of government in which a colony, three thousand distant from the parent state, shall enjoy all the liberty of the parent state."[4]

Oliver and Paxton were even more strident in their notions of what needed to be done in the colony.

Franklin sent the letters to Massachusetts with the understanding that they were to be read by selected colonial leaders but not copied or distributed. Needless to say, they were published, much to Hutchinson's chagrin. To quiet the resulting furor in London over who had given him the letters, Franklin publicly acknowledged he had transmitted them to Massachusetts. Once the source of the letters became known, Franklin was chastised by the Privy Council for the Colonies at a widely attended meeting in January, 1774.

"Franklin was at once dismissed from his office as deputy postmaster-general; and, perceiving that he could no longer be useful, he resigned his agency for Massachusetts."[5] He left England in the spring of 1775 and didn't return until after independence.

Meanwhile, it didn't take Gage long upon his arrival in Boston in 1774 to grasp the political situation and come to the conclusion that the number of troops at his command was totally insufficient to enforce the Coercive Acts.

While the news of Boston's late-night assault was making its way across the Atlantic and the parliamentary reaction making the return voyage, there were even further incidents in emulation of the Boston "Indians." In March of 1774, a similar fate befell a cargo of tea in New York and later that year the *Peggy Stewart* and her tea cargo were burned in Annapolis and some tea storage warehouses in Greenwich, N.J., met a similar fate.

In response to the Coercive Acts, the Massachusetts Committee of Correspondence issued a call in May for an intercolonial meeting to discuss what actions should be taken in the face of the Coercive Acts. Other colonies were quick to respond in the affirmative, led by Providence, Philadelphia and New York before the month was over. By late August, all the colonies except Georgia had named delegates to attend what was to become the first Continental Congress scheduled to be held in Philadelphia in September.

Meanwhile, the Boston merchants reverted to a tried and true retaliation—the Solemn League and Covenant of June, 1774, in which the signatories agreed to end all commerce with Britain effective October 1.

The 55 delegates convened Sept. 5 in the library on the second floor of Philadelphia's Carpenter's Hall and they remained in session nearly seven weeks. Eleven days into their deliberations, Paul Revere arrived from Boston with a copy of the Suffolk Resolves, a set of 19 measures adopted Sept. 9 in a congress of Massachusetts delegates a week earlier. The language was anything but conciliatory.

"If a boundless continent," the resolves said with some clairvoyance, "swarming with millions, will tamely submit to live, move and have their being at the arbitrary will of a licentious minister, they basely yield to voluntary slavery, and future generations shall load their memories with incessant execrations."

The resolves went on to describe the Boston Port Act, the Massachusetts Bay Regulating Act and the Administration of Justice Act as "gross infractions" of both the British constitution and the colony's charter and came to the conclusion "that no obedience is due from this province to either or any part of the acts above-mentioned, but that they be rejected as the attempts of a wicked administration to enslave America."

Residents of the colony were also urged to disregard the judges who held their positions through royal appointment and to hold blameless all sheriffs, deputies and others who refuse to carry out court orders. It also recommended that any tax collector or other officer with public funds in their possession to keep it rather than turn it in to the provincial treasury.

Additional recommendations included the formation of a civilian militia with weekly training sessions; that if patriot leaders were arrested "every servant of the present tyrannical and unconstitutional government" be likewise seized; that goods from Great Britain, Ireland and the West Indies be embargoed; that domestic production of all sorts be promoted, and, perhaps in a warning to the Sons of Liberty, the resolves urged all citizens to refrain from "any routs, riots or licentious attacks on the properties of any person whatsoever."

The confrontational language of the Suffolk Resolves naturally generated much heated discussion among the congressional delegates, but in the end they were endorsed.

But that did not end the division between the conservative and radical components. The First Continental Congress can be looked at as something of a measure of the political maturity of the Northeastern delegates. In the days leading up to the gathering, the conservatives from the middle colonies had been marshalling their forces to counter what they expected to hear from New England. Those delegates, they were sure, would descend on Philadelphia—one of the most conservative cities in one of the most conservative colonies—complete with horns and tails and breathing fire and brimstone.

From the conservatives' point of view, every move was suspect. Even the rejection of Pennsylvania's spacious assembly meeting rooms in favor of Carpenters Hall was interpreted as an attempt to curry favor with labor. When Charles Thomson, who was too radical to be elected a Pennsylvania delegate to the congress, was named secretary, the conservatives—who were even then known as Tories—were further concerned.

But the Tories were disarmed when the New England delegates displayed not a bit of fire and brimstone.

"At the meetings, they were so quiet and unobtrusive that they seemed to have come to Philadelphia solely to enjoy the peace and restful surroundings of the City of Brotherly Love."[6]

What the Tories were not prepared for was the radical attack from the south, notably Virginia and the Carolinas.

"The true fire-eating Whigs seemed to come from south of the Potomac; Christopher Gadsden of South Carolina urged that Gage and the British troops in Boston should be attacked before reinforcements could arrive; Richard Henry Lee of Virginia proposed the Nonimportation and Nonexportation Agreement, and Patrick Henry argued that the empire already was dissolved and that the colonies were in a 'state of nature'."[7]

Five days after the Suffolk Resolves vote, Joseph Galloway, speaker of the Pennsylvania Assembly, presented a proposal for a plan of union between the colonies and Great Britain.

Under the Galloway plan, King George and parliament would continue to regulate the "general affairs of America" but the colonies and their assemblies would administer their own internal affairs. The colonies would be under a royally appointed president-general and a council consisting of representatives elected to three-year terms by the various colonies. The president-general would have veto power over the council.

After nearly a month of arguing over the details, the plan was defeated on Oct. 22 by a vote of six to five.

As the congress wound down its deliberations, the delegates were faced with a delicate balancing act. Its ultimate resolutions must at once not appear too confrontational to the British government and thus close all doors to possible accommodations between American and London, but at the same time satisfy the more radical members of Congress. Care had also to be given not to alienate the sizable ultra-conservative element of the population which had refused to have anything to do with such an extra-legal gathering.

Two things came out of the First Continental Congress—a document called "Declaration and Resolves of the First Continental Congress" and the creation of a voluntary Continental Association, or simply the Association.

To a great extent, the "Declaration and Resolves" were a rehash of arguments that had been advanced before: That British colonists were entitled to the same protection of British laws as those living at home, the Coercive Acts were unconstitutional as were expansion of the Admiralty Courts' jurisdiction, dissolution of colonial assemblies and taxation without representation.

The declaration concluded with the note that "we have, for the present, only resolved to pursue the following peaceable measures: 1. To enter into a non-importation, non-consumption and non-exportation agreement or association. 2. To prepare an address to the people of Great Britain and a memorial to the inhabitants of British America; and, 3. To prepare a loyal address to his majesty, agreeable to resolutions already entered into."

Needless to say, the "loyal address" fell on deaf ears because, as George would write in response to a petition from the pacifist Quakers in September, even before the First Continental Congress adjourned, "The die is now cast. The colonies must either submit or triumph."[8]

"By the end of 1774, unless either the British Government or the colonial leaders capitulated, the chance of avoiding a full-scale conflict looked slender, and to the king, non-existent."[9] Both Gage and Lord North had suggested that negotiation, even repeal of the Coercive Acts be considered, but George would have none of it, at least not until the colonials conceded the supremacy of parliament. Otherwise, it might appear that the government and crown were caving in to violence and a bevy of other illegal acts. To obstinate George, it was now a matter of them or us, and he did not intend that it should be "them."

The memorial to the inhabitants of British America combined with the Association bore more fruit. The Association committed American merchants to the non-importation, non-export, non-consumption resolution. Importation, including slaves, was to cease as of Dec. 1; non-consumption as of March 1, 1775, and non-exportation as of Sept. 1, 1775. The delegates also agreed to meet the following spring if the economic efforts to repeal the Intolerable Acts were unsuccessful.

Tory response to The Association was predictable. They accused those supporting the economic measures as exercising a despotism as bad as the British harshness against which they railed so strongly.

"An American could no longer drink a dish of tea, take a glass of Madeira, or buy an English pin by the edict of this revolutionary body which has usurped authority over British America," they complained.[10]

One of the reasons some of the congressional proposals came to naught was the fact that, although members had agreed to keep their deliberations private, someone among the delegates was keeping the British informed. Although the source was never authenticated, suspicion centers on Dr. Warren.

Through the final two months of 1774 and into 1775, committees were formed in most towns and villages to ensure that local merchants were adhering to provisions of the Association. In the seaports, a system of inspectors was established to keep an eye on incoming shipments and if a violator was discovered his imports were confiscated and his name published.

In most colonies, that is, except in Georgia, which had not sent delegates to the Continental Congress, and in New York, where the assembly declined to ratify The Association and its underlying agreements. New Yorkers did, however, adopt a resolution similar to that which had come out of the congressional meeting. It was forwarded to their agent in London, Edmund Burke, but it "was found to be so emphatic in its claims of rights that the ministers opposed and prevented its reception."[11]

Along with the commercial agreements, the colonies were encouraged to promote and patronize colonial producers and manufacturers and, of course, boycott any offending merchant. Persistent offenders were liable for a coat of tar and feathers.

The other two were more effective By November, 1774, the king was declaring "The New England governments are in a state of rebellion."[12]

George's entrenched position against any sort of conciliatory measures left both the royally appointed officials and that portion of the general populace still loyal to the crown in a rather awkward position. Increasingly, they sought refuge in those areas with a strong presence of British troops. The population of Boston and New York swelled accordingly.

As the colonists under the leadership of the Association began mustering and training militia companies and accumulating arms and powder right under the noses of the British, tensions naturally increased while overcrowding, unemployment and food shortages did little to raise the mood in the peninsula that was Boston.

On the first of February, 1775, Pitt made his last effort to head off what he saw as an inevitable conflict by proposing a Provisional Act under which the Continental Congress would be recognized and granted wide powers, although under the general authority of parliament. No revenues would be raised in the colonies without their consent, but in return the colonies would raise a revenue for the crown. The plan was turned down by the House of Lords

Later the same month, Lord North ushered a "Conciliatory Resolution" through Parliament in a vague gesture to appease the colonies that promised "to forbear" from the imposition of "any duty, tax or assessment" on any colony that would provide "their proportion to the common defense . . . and shall engage to make provision also for the support of the civil government, and the administration of justice . . ."

Even as he was extending this rather tenuous olive branch, parliament was hard at work on the New England Trade and Fisheries Act, more popularly known as the New England Restraining Act. In introducing the measure, North held that "as the Americans has refused to trade with this kingdom. It was but just that we should not suffer then to trade with any other nation." [13]

Debate began in February and was to consume some two months, but it passed with royal approval at the end of March, 1775. It was during this debate that Edmund Burke delivered his famed speech urging conciliation, but to no avail.

The Restraining Act was parliament's own response to the colonial non-trade agreement adopted at the First Continental Congress. The act as originally drawn would forbid the New England colonies from dealing with any country but England as opposed to the colonial embargo that permitted trade with virtually every country except England.

The ban was to take effect July 1 and on July 20 New England fishermen were to be banned from the Newfoundland Banks, the main North Atlantic fishery.

While the debate was in progress, however, word was received in London of the ratification by 11 of the 13 colonies of the Continental Association created during the First

Continental Congress. North then introduced an amendment that extended the act to include all the colonies but New York and Georgia, the two non-signers, and North Carolina, which the ministers still thought might be won to the Tory side. The amendment passed parliament in mid-April.

Only a day after the Restraining Act was adopted, Gen. Gage received an order dated in late January from William Legge, Earl of Dartmouth and current secretary of state for the colonies, directing him to enforce the Coercive Acts with force.

In the light of all the military preparations going on around him, he realized the fact that by late 1774 he was in a no-win situation. Under orders to enforce the Coercive Acts, he recognized he had not enough forces to face a determined rebellion.

Gage was not an adept politician, but he did his best to maintain control over the troops and sought to lend an attentive ear to the Whigs. In his early dealings with the colonists, he drew criticism from the hard line Tories as being too soft on the Americans.

As commander-in-chief, however, he could not turn a blind eye to what was going on around him during the winter of 1774-75. Militias were being trained, guns and ammunition being stored up, resistance was being preached from the pulpits and British troops hardly dared venture outside Boston.

As governor of Massachusetts Bay Colony as well as commander-in-chief of British forces in America, he had naturally kept London informed as to the situation brewing in Massachusetts.

Writing to the government in November, 1774, he tried to present what he considered a realistic evaluation.

"If force is to be used at length, it must be a considerable one for to begin with small numbers will encourage resistance and not terrify; and in the end will cost more blood and treasure."[14]

So great was the sense of superiority in London that Gage's request for reinforcements was seen as cowardice and led to demands for his recall.

In late February, British troops had landed at Salem with the intention of seizing gunpowder and other militia military stores and in March some 13,000 cartridges being smuggled out of Boston were seized. Fortifications were constructed across Boston Neck, the narrowest part of the peninsula that was Boston, projecting essentially north into Boston harbor.

Word of the Salem raid spread rapidly throughout the colonies and the various assemblies met hastily to decide on a response. It was in late March, during a meeting of the Virginia House of Burgesses, that Patrick Henry delivered his "Give me liberty or give me death" speech.

April, 1775, as most schoolchildren are aware, thanks in part to the poet Longfellow, was a pivotal time in the history of the country. Word reached Boston on April 2 that British reinforcements were en route to Boston and there were those who argued that the British, pretty well bottled up in the city behind fortifications erected on the Neck the year before, should be attacked before the reinforcements arrived. In keeping with the pronouncements from the First Continental Congress, which appeared to condone only defensive military action, the idea was defeated.

Meanwhile, Gage was under orders from England to enforce the Coercive Acts. He had intelligence that the colonials had secreted gunpowder at Concord and, as a bonus he was informed that both Hancock and Sam Adams, for whom he had arrest warrants, were in nearby Lexington.

Forewarned by a source inside the colonial ranks that the colonials were prepared to meet force with force, Gage mounted what was to have been a clandestine operation. He dispatched an 800-man party to Concord and Lexington but word was out and, in response to the famous "one if by land, two if by sea" signal, William Dawes and Paul Revere set off to spread the alarm. They were aided by a three-hour delay while soaking wet troops waited for provisions to be landed and distributed before setting off on their 12-mile march. They arrived in Lexington about 5 a.m. to be greeted by 60 to 70 militiamen assembled on the common in response to the alarm of Revere and Dawes.

More than 200 years after the event, there is no definitive explanation of what happened next. There were orders from the British to disperse, which apparently some of the minutemen attempted to do. Each side argues that the other side fired first. Paul Revere, who was in Lexington, related later that he was close enough to hear the shots, but was busy salvaging a trunk of John Hancock's papers from an inn and never actually saw the encounter. Other accounts differ, depending on whether the author was American or English.

One account, attributed to Lt. John Barker of the King's Own, notes that after the exchange of gunfire that wounded one British trooper, "We waited a considerable time, and at length proceeded on our way to Concord, which we then learnt was our destination, in order to destroy a magazine of stores collected there."[15] The lieutenant estimated the colonial dead at Lexington as some 60 Minutemen and another 10 wounded. The count, most agree, was about eight killed and 10 wounded.

Moving on toward Concord, the lieutenant continues, "We met with no interruption till within a mile or two of the town, where the country people had occupied a hill which commanded the road." The locals retreated three times in the face of the advancing British until they were across the river on the far side of Concord.

By now, a sizable force of militia—perhaps as many as 1,000—had converged on Concord and took up positions on a rise overlooking the bridge, taking shelter behind a stone wall. The company of British guarding the bridge called for reinforcements and two additional companies joined, taking positions on the far side of the bridge. The two forces stared each other down for the better part of an hour.

At length, the colonials began to advance down the hill toward the British, who were forced to beat an unorganized retreat across the bridge. With an exchange of fire, the militia forced its way across the bridge but, with the arrival of additional British troops, they retired across the bridge once more. The British retired into Concord with four officers wounded, three troopers killed and several wounded.

Their mission conceded to be completed, the British column started its march back to Boston. It was a trying experience. After a century of fighting Indians, the Americans employed the same tactics against the British column, taking advantage of every tree and stonewall. Under constant sniping, the column made about 10 miles before meeting a relief column sent from Boston.

Approaching Boston, the lieutenant reported, "We were now obliged to force almost every house in the road, for the rebels had taken possession of them and galled us exceedingly; but they suffered for their temerity, for all that were found in the houses were put to death."

The British reached the relative safety of the Charlestown shores of Boston harbor between 7 and 8 p.m., where they awaited the boats to bring them across to Boston, ending a 20-hour odyssey that, according to the lieutenant, "from beginning to end was as ill planned and ill executed as it is possible to be."[16] British losses were estimated at 250 dead, wounded or missing.

Gage, in a dispatch dated April 22 to Lord Barrington, Secretary of War, dismissed the action rather matter of factly. "I have now nothing to trouble your Lordship with, but an affair that happened here on the 19th instant."

Taken at its face, it would appear that Gage didn't realize that the first battle of the Revolution had been fought.

Chapter 16

There were others, however, who were more perceptive, both here and abroad.

When the news broke in London, particularly the colonial version that arrived first, it nearly led to the overthrow of the North administration. Horace Walpole in commenting in a letter to Sir Horace Mann clearly recognized the encounter as the first act of "this fatal war."[1]

To the colonials, Lexington and Concord were a propaganda bonanza. The British had gone 12 miles out into the countryside to seize property of the colony and in the effort had—in the colonists' eyes at least—fired the first shots and cleared the way for the defensive war condoned by the First Continental Congress.

Horror stories abounded. The colonials talked in great detail about mothers and daughters bayoneted or burned to death in their homes. The British were equally expressive in describing scalpings and other mutilations inflicted on the dead and wounded.

The colonial version of events also reached the other colonies long before the official British version, leading Gage to claim the revolutionaries had interfered with the mail in order to delay the British account from being published. In fact, the colonial version reached North Carolina a full two months before the British version, dealing a severe blow to the Tory cause in that colony.

Through the second half of April and into June, militia from Massachusetts and surrounding colonies massed in ever greater numbers at the foot of the peninsula that was Boston.

One thing the encircling militia lacked was sufficient artillery to seriously threaten the British bottled up on the peninsula. Almost simultaneously, it occurred to both the Massachusetts and Connecticut Committees of Safety that there was artillery to be had at the rather isolated British outpost of Fort Ticonderoga at the foot of Lake Champlain. Without possible reinforcement from Boston, the small garrison should not be much of an obstacle.

Both committees commissioned attacks on the fort, with the Connecticut contingent headed by Ethan Allen of the New Hampshire Grants (later Vermont) and Benedict Arnold as head of the Massachusetts effort. Arnold, without any forces, met Allen, backed by between 200 and 300 men, at the lake in early May. Arnold and Allen argued about who should be in charge, but finally compromised on joint command.

On the night of May 9, the two commanders along with some 80 men crossed the lake and at dawn surprised the fort, which fell without a shot being fired. The raid netted some 100 cannon as well as a sizable cache of military supplies. To complete the sweep of British forces in the area, Arnold went on a few miles north to capture the 13-man Crown Point garrison and, commandeering the only British ship on the lake, sailed further north to take St. Johns, an outpost just over the border in Canada. The 60-man garrison headed by Capt. William Delaplace, along with those captured at Crown Point and St. John, were marched to Hartford, Conn., by way of Albany, N.Y.

Ironically, one of those captured at St. Johns and marched south was a second lieutenant named John Andre, the same

John Andre whose name was to become forever linked with Arnold's in the young country's most notable case of treason.

While they were small actions from a military standpoint, they accomplished two strategic objectives: they gained needed supplies and cut off any possible overland support from British troops in Canada for the immediate future.

Meanwhile, the Second Continental Congress convened in early May at Philadelphia. Delegates found themselves faced with a far different scenario than they had anticipated six months earlier. Not only had their economic measures failed to force repeal of the Coercive Acts, resolution not to make any concessions to the colonies had crystallized in London. There had now been open armed conflict at Lexington, Concord and on the shores of Lake Champlain and thousands of militia were laying siege to Boston.

The congress was to remain in virtually continuous session for the next six years. Initially, it acted in an advisory capacity to the individual colonies—advising New York to arm and train a militia in event the British should attempt to take the principal city and advising Massachusetts to set up its government as it had been "until a governor, of his majesty's appointment, will consent to govern the colony according to its charter." [2]

While the Second Continental Congress was charting its course in the face on the facts on the ground, the British situation in Boston was changing. On May 25, 1775, after 34 days at sea, His Majesty's Ship *Cerebus* arrived in Boston carrying three top-ranking major generals to take charge of affairs in the colonies. Heading the military trio was Sir William Howe, accompanied by Sir Henry Clinton and General John Burgoyne. Howe had served in America under Gen. James Wolfe during the capture of Quebec and Clinton, son of a British admiral, was born in America.

They were accompanied by some 2,000 troops, bringing the British total in the city to between 6,000 to 8,000 while some 16,000 colonial militiamen encircled the city from the Mystic River to the north to Dorchester on the south.

With blood shed at Lexington and Concord, and military operations around Lake Champlain, matters had deteriorated to the point where delegates in Philadelphia were forced to shift their focus to a more national scope when faced with the proposition that a national army should be raised.

Congressional delegates elected to adopt the force already arrayed before Boston and, following a suggestion by John Adams, on June 14 Col. George Washington of Virginia was unanimously selected as its commanding general.

Two days before Washington's appointment and five days before the Battle of Bunker Hill, Gen. Gage issued a proclamation (probably written by published playwright Burgoyne) in which he "in his Majesty's name, offer and promise his most gracious pardon to all persons who shall forthwith lay down their arms and return to their duties of peaceable subjects, excepting only from the benefit of such pardon Samuel Adams and John Hancock, whose offenses are of too flagitious a nature to admit of any other consideration than that of condign punishment." Those who saw fit not to take advantage of this "gracious pardon" were held "to be rebels and traitors, and as such to be treated."[3]

Given the situation on the ground, one might be tempted to call the proclamation somewhat audacious, to say nothing of useless, particularly the proclamation's assertion that the colonials "who with a preposterous parade of military arrangement, affected to hold the army besieged."[4] It was readily recognized in London that the army was, in fact, besieged.

Gage's proclamation was something of a bluff, as indicated by a letter he wrote Lord North in London on the same day he issued the proclamation. In his letter, Gage painted a more realistic picture of his situation.

"The situation these wretches have taken in forming the blockade of this town is judicious and strong, being well intrenched where the situation requires it and with cannon."

Meanwhile, his position was precarious. "In our present state all warlike preparations are wanting." No maps, no boats, no horses, no forage, no wagons.

Naturally, the newly arrived trio of generals individually acknowledged the same thing in their correspondence and blamed Gage for not making the proper preparations. For the most part, the accusations were true, but given the circumstances, his lack of military action was understandable. A year earlier, he had been required to enforce the parliamentary act closing the port of Boston, an act that quickly eroded whatever good will he had among the colony's residents. Fear of arousing an already antagonistic population stayed his hand and, as in the Concord and Lexington raids, he acted only on direct orders from London. The Concord and Lexington raid had also demonstrated his inability to carry out any sort of secret maneuver.

But the British were going to try anyway. It didn't take the triumvirate of new generals long to realize that the city would be vulnerable if the overlooking hills of Charlestown to the north and Dorchester to the south were to be occupied by the rebels. Together they hatched a plan to attack the rebel headquarters of Gen. Artemus Ward in Cambridge and at the same time send detachments to occupy the heights in Charlestown and Dorchester. Date of the campaign was to be June 18.

Naturally, word of the plan inevitably leaked to the colonials and on the night of June 16 some 1,200 men were dispatched to occupy Breed's Hill, a slightly lower elevation to the south of Bunker Hill in Charlestown. The British awoke the morning of June 17 to discover a rude set of breastworks looking down on the town.

Behind the makeshift fortifications stood some 1,500 to 1,700 militiamen, dangerously short of food, water and ammunition. With several warships in the harbor, including the *Glasgow*, *Somerset* and *Lively* along with smaller gunboats, and with the rebels perched on the tip of a peninsula not unlike that of Boston itself, an encircling maneuver would have undoubtedly made short work of the engagement.

That was Clinton's recommendation, but Gage vetoed the move, certain that a frontal assault would quickly dislodge the rebels.

Despite the extremely hot June weather, despite the fact that the troops had to cross only a short distance from their base and regardless of Gage's anticipation of a short engagement, the 2,000 troops ferried across in barges were loaded down with full regalia—heavy tunics, rolled blankets and three days' food ration. In the face of common sense, the standard battle preparations must be taken.

By 3 p.m., preparations were complete, including the additional reinforcements Howe called for almost immediately after his initial force landed. Up the hill the troops started, but they were soon under musket fire from the town of Charlestown, which had been essentially abandoned as being within easy range of the cannon aboard the British warships. Howe sent word back to Burgoyne to set fire to Charlestown, and soon the 300 to 400 houses were alight.

Burgoyne later wrote that as the first troops ascended the hill "they met with a thousand impediments from strong fences and were much exposed."[5]

With admirable restraint, the colonials held their fire until the British were at point-blank range. The withering fire sent them back down the hill. Reforming in a line, the redcoats made a second assault, again under the leadership of Howe, but with the same result.

Clinton, watching the engagement from Boston, realized the difficulties Howe was having. Acting without orders from Gage, he rounded up another 500 soldiers and crossed to the Charlestown side. With the added manpower and the remaining troops stripped of their packs, Howe marshaled a third assault. With the defenders on the heights running low on ammunition, the British managed to get within bayonet range and those colonials who remained were forced to take to their heels.

Fortunately, a relief party had taken up positions to the rear of Bunker Hill and its rearguard action held until the last of the colonials had crossed the causeway. There was no pursuit on the part of the fatigued and much diminished British.

Since he ended up in possession of the field at the end of the day, Howe was entitled to claim victory, but it was a victory dearly bought. Gage's official report listed the dead and wounded at 1,741, including 24 dead officers. Why historians would question the official count and hold out for about 1,000 dead and wounded is anyone's guess. But even the lower number constituted some 40 percent of the British forces engaged.

Colonial losses were set at about 450, including Dr. Joseph Warren, president of the Massachusetts Provincial Congress, who was among the last to leave the redoubt.

It has been argued that the heavy costs of the battle significantly altered Howe's future campaigns against Washington's forces throughout the Revolution—that he would never again venture a frontal attack because of the heavy losses sustained in Charlestown.

William Howe, as commander-in-chief of the British land forces in America, and his brother Admiral Richard "Black Dick" Howe, as commander of His Majesty's navy, were a strange pair to be heading the military efforts.

Both Howes, along with a third brother, George Augustus, had served with distinction in America during the Seven Years War in operations against the French, primarily in Canada. George Augustus was killed at the battle of Ticonderoga in 1758. He was held in such regard by the colonists that the Massachusetts Assembly voted £250 to raise a monument to him in Westminster Abbey.

Both William and Richard were members of parliament, William succeeding his decreased brother, from Nottingham and William had broken with Grenville administration over its harsh American policies. He voted against prosecuting Wilkes and against the Stamp Act. As late as 1774, when running for reelection, he criticized the American policies as "too harsh" and pledged to vote to repeal the Massachusetts Acts and that he would not command against the colonists.

It should be noted that in most instances, William's votes followed those of his older brother.

Lord George Germain, then Secretary of State for the American Colonies, was convinced that Howe's "names as well as abilities would be instrumental to restore discipline and confidence" in Massachusetts.[6] Howe reluctantly went back on his election pledge when faced with the choice of duty to country and affection for America.

It has also been reasoned that he saw the assignment as a way of controlling and implementing British policy in America. Knowing that Gage was unpopular at home, it was not too much of a stretch to see himself elevated to Gage's position as commander-in-chief, which is just what happened only months after he arrived in Boston.

Throughout the summer and fall of 1775, there were still hopes by some on both sides that matters could be resolved peacefully—or at least with no more bloodshed than there had already been. On July 5, Congress in Philadelphia adopted what is called the Olive Branch Petition setting out means whereby the differences between the colonies and mother country might be resolved.

The petition was the colonists' last attempt to find a conciliatory solution to the differences between them and their mother country. Composed by John Dickinson, congressional delegate from Pennsylvania, the petition was forwarded in part to appease those in Congress still resisting the idea of independence. In it, Dickinson sought to assert the rights of the colonists while at the same time maintaining their loyalty to the crown.

The rather lengthy petition placed blame for the current situation on "the irksome variety of artifices practiced by many of your Majesty's ministers" and concluded by imploring George "to direct some mode by which the united applications of your faithful colonists to the throne . . . may be improved into a happy and permanent reconciliation; and that in the meantime measures be taken for preventing the further destruction of the lives of your Majesty's subjects; and that such statutes as more immediately distress any of your Majesty's colonies be repealed."

Three days later, two copies of the petition were dispatched by separate ships—one carried by Richard August Penn, former Pennsylvania governor, and the second by Arthur Lee. Arriving safely in London, Penn and Lee arranged to have a copy transmitted to Lord Dartmouth, Secretary of State for the Colonies, and a date set for formal presentation. On Sept. 2, Penn and Lee reported to Congress that they had been informed that George would not accept the petition and "no answer would be given."

The response, received late in the year, virtually eliminated whatever resistance to independence that might still be found among the delegates in Philadelphia.

In England, however, George's response prompted a heated debate when Parliament convened in late October. There were many voices raised in opposition to the seemingly inevitable war in North America, including Rockingham, Shelburne, Burke and Barre. They also had the support of the merchants and other commercial interests who stood to lose mightily in any cut off of colonial trade.

Writing in opposition to the Massachusetts Government Act in May, 1774, the Bishop of Asaph offered the opinion that "By enslaving your colonies, you not only ruin the peace, the commerce and the fortunes of both countries, but you extinguish the fairest hopes, shut up the last asylum of mankind."[7] In January, 1775, Pitt (now Lord Chatham) warned parliament during the debate on withdrawing troops from Boston that Americans "prefer poverty with liberty to gilded chains and sordid affluence." Military measures to enforce obedience, Burke said, is "but a feeble instrument for preserving a people so numerous, so active, so growing, so spirited as this, in a profitable and subordinate connexion with us."

All such proposals for a peaceful settlement with the colonies fell on deaf ears. Proposals by Chatham were voted down in the House of Lords 68-18 and 61-32 while Burke's plan was defeated 271-78 in the House of Commons. Parliament was not in a conciliatory mood.

At the time, the British army numbered some 48,000, one-quarter occupied in "pacifying" the Irish, while Gage was estimating his manpower requirements at about 32,000, about five times the number he had at his disposal.[8] Seymour[9] gives essentially the same figure, listing some 15,000 posted in England, 12,000 in Ireland and 8,500 in America.

There were those in the administration and in the military—albeit a minority—who felt that under the circumstances such a land war was, in the words of Gen. Edward Harvey, "as wild an idea as ever controverted common sense."[10]

In response to events in North America, parliament agreed to increase the army strength to 55,000, but the question remained—Where were the additional soldiers to come from? The answer had to be mercenaries, a common practice in Europe for centuries.

While Holland and Russia refused to hire out any of their troops, the various German princes were only too willing. British troops at Gibraltar and Minorca were replaced with mercenaries and still more were hired for service in America. "Altogether, these German princes contributed nearly 30,000 men for service in America."[11]

Among the alternatives suggested to a land war was a

naval blockade of the Atlantic coast, but that had only one drawback—the navy was in no better shape for that undertaking than the army was for a land war. Rather than investing in the navy, succeeding administrations were more concerned with the national debt from the Seven Years War and had concentrated more on keeping taxes down. Once more, domestic political considerations had taken primacy.

By 1771, when Lord Sandwich became First Lord of the Admiralty, the British navy had shrunk to 18,000 men and the ships were mostly in bad condition.

"In 1775, limited impressments was allowed and the navy's strength on paper was increased to 28,000 men."[12]

Even at this late hour, Burke introduced a measure in parliament that might have at least delayed open revolution by renouncing taxation and repealing the revenue measures that had so angered the Americans. It was defeated by 100 votes.[13]

Not only was Burke's conciliatory measure defeated, Parliament further displayed its split personality by passing even more restrictive measures while at the same time appointing a two-man peace commission "empowered to offer pardons and discuss conciliation with Congress."[14] Selected as the commissioners were none other than Gen. Howe, commander-in-chief of the land forces, and his brother, Admiral Lord Howe, commander of the naval forces.

The division also led to a shakeup in the Privy Council. The Duke of Grafton resigned as Privy Seal; North's half-brother, Lord Dartmouth was dismissed as Secretary of State for the American Colonies for being considered too slow to act and too soft on the Americans. He was replaced by George Sackville, now Lord Germain, who had been disgraced at the Battle of Minden 16 years before and declared "unfit to serve his Majesty in any military capacity whatsoever."[15] Germain was also named Privy Seal. He was a hardliner intent on recovering his reputation but he had few friends among the military.

"There were five principal British generals in North America between 1775 and 1781—Howe, (Guy) Carleton, Clinton, Burgoyne and Cornwallis. Germain began bitterly at odds with the first two and ended at daggers drawn with all but Cornwallis: and even Cornwallis was critical."[16] "Lord George Germain, the Secretary of State for the Colonies, had not spoken to Howe's brother, the admiral, for seventeen years."[17]

Germain may have been thought a strange selection to such a powerful post, but what more faithful servant could be found than one who owes the opportunity to regain his honor to his master?

Unfortunately, Germain was a meddler with his generals and field commanders, sometimes bypassing the commander-in-chief to issue instructions. Given his antipathy toward the Howe brothers, this was not unexpected.

As winter of 1775-76 approached, the government suggested Howe move his troops to loyalist laden Long Island where, it was believed, they would be welcomed more warmly than they were in Boston and could more easily be supplied.

Howe answered that he had not sufficient transport, that two trips would be required, leaving a reduced garrison in between trips that would invite possible assault by the besiegers. And so Howe sat in a besieged city for nearly nine months in what became an increasingly untenable military position. The colonials camped in his doorstep had all the resources of food and provisions available through overland routes from not only Massachusetts but also surrounding colonies. Howe's only supply line stretched 3,000 miles across the Atlantic. On the other end of that supply line, the administration could not understand how a pack of rabble could possibly withstand what they felt was the finest army in the world, particularly since reinforcements arrived in both September and December.

Two days before Congress penned its last petition to the throne Washington arrived in Boston to take command of the army. With Howe seemingly content to remain passive, Washington put the time to good use training and drilling the militiamen, although they had a tendency to drift away home when they felt they had devoted enough time to the siege. Installation of order and discipline, however, sometimes required the lash and even the gallows.

With the British bottled up in Boston, the colonials were also free to conduct military operations in other areas of the country—which they did.

In September, Gen. Richard Montgomery moved northward out of Fort Ticonderoga with some 2,000 men and by November had taken possession of Montreal. Washington sent Gen. Benedict Arnold north with another 1,100 men to join Montgomery on the banks of the St. Lawrence River in November.

On New Year's Eve, they made a combined, ill-fated assault on Quebec. Montgomery was killed in the battle, Arnold wounded and Ethan Allen taken prisoner, to spend the rest of the war in England.

At Boston, Washington met a 25-year-old bookseller of the city named Henry Knox, a self-educated expert in artillery. Knox suggested that the nearly 60 canon captured at Fort Ticonderoga certainly would be handy in laying siege to Boston. Convinced by Knox that it could be done, Washington commissioned him a colonel and sent him with a party to get it done. Included in the original train were 82 sleds, 160 oxen and more than 125 horses.[18]

Knox proved to be a logistical genius as well as an outstanding artillery officer. In later years, Knox was to orchestrate the army's crossing of the Delaware to surprise the Hessians in Trenton.

The hauling of the cannon back to Boston by ox-drawn sledges, which required some 75 days, is one of the more heroic incidents of the period. Knox arrived back in Boston March 1, 1776, giving Washington the chance to break the deadlock with Howe. Under cover of a cannonade from their

Roxbury positions, Washington moved some 2,000 troops the night of March 4 to the south, occupying Dorchester Heights. Throughout the night they dug, as they had on Breed's Hill, and moved the cannon into place.

"The night was remarkably mild, a finer for working could not have been taken out of the whole 365," the Rev. William Gordon wrote. "It was hazy below so that our people could not be seen, tho' it was a bright moon light night above on the hills."[19]

As they had been the previous year at Bunker Hill, the British were totally surprised at the view of a bristling Dorchester Heights when they saw it in the morning.

The heights commanded an excellent view of the city and Howe was not slow to grasp the significance of the situation. Boston was no longer defensible.

"Howe briefly considered an attack, but soon decided it was best to bargain. He proposed that in return for his safe departure from Boston, he would not raze the city."[20] The offer was made under a flag of truce, according to Col. Charles Stuart in a letter to Lord Bute.[21] Washington accepted.

Orders for the evacuation were given March 7 and another 10 days were required to load everything—and everyone—aboard the ships. On Sunday, March 17, the ships hoisted anchor and stood out to sea. The flotilla lay off Nantasket for another five days while cargo, provisions and passengers were shifted in preparation for the coming voyage.

As Howe wrote the Earl of Dartmouth while lying at anchor after evacuating the city, fortification of Dorchester Heights left him with the little choice but to evacuate. No supplies had been received either from the southern colonies or the West Indies, Howe wrote, and Washington's move "has reduced me to the necessity either of exposing the army to the greater distress by remaining in Boston, or of withdrawing from it under such straitened conditions."[22]

Howe had another surprise for London. Rather than

heading south for Long Island he headed north for Halifax. London's advice to go south was based on the notion that that area was swarming with Loyalists who would give him and his charges a warm welcome and support. From Howe's view point, given the condition of his forces after months of siege and the number of civilians taken aboard, he was in no position to withstand any hostile opposition to a Long Island landing. At least in Halifax there was a British garrison.

According to Gen. Howe's report to the Earl of Dartmouth, "Such military stores as could not be taken on board were destroyed," but a selectman of Boston reported that "A number of loaded shells with trains of powder covered with straw were found in houses left by the Regulars near the fortifycation." [23]

Arriving at Halifax in late March, Howe unloaded his civilian passengers and paused to rest and refurbish his troops

While Howe rested in Nova Scotia, Washington and the Congress were quick to perceive that Howe's next move would be to try to take New York, renewing an old strategy of splitting off New England from the remainder of the colonies.

"Choked and detached, New England would barely be capable of defending itself against an invasion from New York, the final act in the destruction of the American rebellion."[24]

It seemed rather obvious that with British control in Canada and New York connected by the Hudson River and Lake Champlain, the entire colonial confederation would be seriously weakened and the British could use New York harbor as a base to mount a blockade of the New England coast.

Only weeks after the British evacuation of Boston, Washington headed south to begin fortifications around the city and on Long Island in anticipation of a spring attack. He had less than five months to do the job.

Meanwhile, at home, there were still political divisions. In addition to colonial defenders in parliament, the commercial interests were divided on the economic consequences of what they perceived as a civil war with about three million of their best customers. It was argued by some that the mother country would derive far more in revenue from the American colonies through free trade than it ever would by enforced taxation.

There was an even stronger concern on the part of politicians if the situation devolved into a full-scale rebellion, something that the colonists had already hinted at—foreign intervention.

The defeat of France and Spain in the Seven Years War 13 years earlier was only the latest in a long competition between England and the European powers, and neither of the Catholic kingdoms had either forgotten or forgiven.

"With fears of French intervention growing, the idea of a peace commission appealed strongly to North"[25] and despite the skepticism of His Majesty, appointed Gen. Howe and Admiral Howe as a two-man delegation to pursue the possibility with Gen. Washington even while they were charged with the conduct of military operations against the troops under his command.

Howe's fleet started appearing off New York at the end of June. He set foot on Staten Island July 2, the very day that Congress in Philadelphia was ratifying the Declaration of Independence.

Throughout the remainder of June, the month of July and into August the British forces continued to gather in New York harbor. Finally on Aug. 22, Howe made his move and invaded Long Island with some 32,000 regulars and Hessians. Washington had divided his forces between Manhattan island and Long Island. The Long Island forces were soon out flanked and forced to withdraw, escaping from both Manhattan and Long Island under the cover of darkness.

Firmly in control of their immediate objective, the Howe brothers turned to their other mission—trying to reach come accommodation with the Americans.

In July, the admiral sent a dispatch to Washington's camp under a flag of truce addressed to "George Washington, Esquire." "Of course, Washington refused to receive a communication which did not recognize his official position."[26] He had, in fact, ordered his delegates—Col. Henry Knox, Col. Joseph Reed and Lt. Col. Samuel Webb—not to accept any correspondence not properly addressed. A second effort, delivered this time by the Gen. Howe's adjutant-general identified by Knox as Colonel Paterson,[27] led to a face-to-face audience with Washington. Addressed "George Washington, etc., etc., etc" the bearer fared no better, even though he explained that the "etc., etc., etc." might be translated as Washington's official title.

"He said the 'etc., etc.' implied everything. 'It does so,' said the general 'and anything'."[28] The meeting, though fruitless, was extremely civil, complete with refreshments. At length, explaining that the Howe brothers were waiting for him to dine aboard the man of war *Eagle*, Paterson took his leave.

"Baffled in his efforts, Lord Howe and his brother determined to begin hostilities."[29]

In early September, colonial Gen. John Sullivan appeared in Philadelphia after being paroled by the British to bring the congress word that Howe wanted to parley.

The proposal spawned considerable debate among the delegates, many of whom sensed a trap or an effort to drive a wedge between the colonies. After four days of discussion, Congress appointed John Adams, Benjamin Franklin and Edward Rutledge to meet with Admiral Howe Sept. 11 on Staten Island. Gen. Howe even called a cessation in operations while his brother met with the congressional delegation.

The half-hearted attempt was, of course, doomed to failure because the terms Howe was empowered to offer—and already understood—were far below what the colonists were disposed to accept.

At the outset, Howe conceded "All would have been better

had he only arrived before the Declaration of Independence which 'changed the ground'."[30]

He also cautioned the trio that he could not deal with them as representatives of a Congress which His Majesty did not recognize but "merely as gentlemen of great ability and influence."[31] "It had soon become obvious that Howe had no authority other than to grant pardons should America submit which, as Franklin told him, meant he had nothing really to offer." [32]

Perhaps what Howe did not tell the delegation was that Adams was not among those who would receive His Majesty's gracious pardon. "He was to hang."[33]

Perhaps what Franklin did not tell Howe was that he had been in contact with the French foreign minister Varennes some four months earlier and Congress had dispatched Silas Deane to France to initiate what turned into a two-and-a-half year effort to enlist that country's support.

It was the last effort by either side to seek a political solution to their disagreements.

What was to follow was seven years of armed conflict in which the pendulum of fate swung first one way and then another. Volumes have been written on individual days, battles and campaigns that transpired until the final peace treaty of 1783.

But the author has reached his self-assigned terminus—ratification of the Declaration of Independence. All that remains is to revisit our original premise to see whether we gained any ground toward answering the questions that littered the mental landscape.

Epilogue

And so, where has this sometimes meandering review of the immediate pre-Revolutionary period led the author—and perhaps the reader?

It seems to the author that the period was a prime example of a principal unknown, or at least, unenunciated, at the time—the law of unintended consequences.

Much of what happened in the colonies between 1763 and 1776 was the byproduct of events that had very little to do directly with the colonies.

Let us look at the three threads mentioned at the outset—commerce, religion and politics.

The commercial pattern which was to become known as mercantilism was set long before there were any British colonies in America. Beginning in the 1400s, all the seafaring nations of Europe—England, France, Spain and Portugal—each started carving out their little corners of the world and were set on defending them with force as best they could. The Netherlands was a slightly different case. Unable to compete militarily with its larger neighbors, it sought to become the commercial carrier for the world and. as a result, became the commercial competitor for the world.

The intentions of the British Acts of Navigation, like similar acts of other countries, were exclusionary. They were adopted to prevent other countries from competing in the British home market or to gain a share of what competing commerce that might be allowed by interposing themselves in the distribution system. But in each case, the reason was the same—profit.

In time, that exclusion came to be internal as well as external.

As noted in Chapter 1, the overall mercantilist philosophy was the same—sell as much as possible, buy as little as possible and so get rich on the difference. By the time for first English colony was planted in Virginia, the pattern was well-established. Several wars had been fought to solidify the structure.

But the English colonies in North America did not start any of these wars nor were they started because of the North American colonies. What military action that might have occurred in America was an offshoot of the European conflicts.

As each of the larger states gained in strength—France, Spain and finally England—the trading networks of both Portugal and The Netherlands were taken over to the greater enrichment of the other three.

Victory in the Seven Years War—what has been called the great war for empire—left England master of all she surveyed in 1763, her mercantilist policies still in place.

In 1763, only two British possessions posed any major economic threat to British home industries—Ireland and the North American colonies.

Caribbean islands were essentially agricultural economies, sources for crops that could not be grown in England. India, despite its teeming population, exported only its unique products such as spices and textiles.

Ireland, sharing the same geographic conditions as England, grew what was grown in England. With its livestock production, agricultural products and textile trade, it competed with many English interests.

Being an island and in close proximity to England, it was no great feat to clamp an effective surveillance to ensure that the various trade regulations imposed by parliament were observed, much to the detriment of the Irish.

With the North American colonies. however, control and enforcement was a quite different problem, which the British could never quite understand.

Which may be understandable. England had been building her mercantilist structure for more than a century. From her standpoint, it worked well enough. There was no room for compromise without endangering the entire structure.

Part of what the English did not understand was that for that same century a society was growing on the other side of the ocean under a completely different environment. While it might be developing under the mercantilist system as far as international trade was concerned, it was also developing domestically into a free market society.

The problem became insoluble when the navigation acts were converted into revenue acts. But again, the reason for this attempted conversion was domestic—the massive debt England had sustained in the successful prosecution of the Seven Years War.

Religion in England was a bloody affair from the time of Henry VIII until the Act of Settlement in 1701

The ever-swinging pendulum between Catholicism and Protestantism provided the impetus for the exodus to North America in the 1600s. But once again, the question of religion was a domestic matter in England. Dissenters like the Puritans and Pilgrims picked up their religion and moved to get away from the controversy.

In the nearly 150 years between the founding of Plymouth and the Treaty of Paris, colonials of various religious convictions managed to coexist with a reasonable degree of pacificity. With plenty of elbow room on a virgin continent, as noted, disagreements that might have caused physical confrontation in England usually led to the establishment of a new colony in North America.

Protestantism was fairly homogenous from North to South with the exception of the Quakers in Pennsylvania and Catholics in Maryland, but politically even they considered themselves English subjects. If matters of religion played a major role in the events between 1763 and 1776, it is not overtly apparent.

"The only organic and official action taken by a religious denomination in behalf of the American cause was that of the Presbyterians, who delegated the only minister to the Congress of 1776 to give their vote for independence."[1]

Which brings us to politics.

Few periods of English history have drawn more study—and more controversy—that the early years of George III's reign. Whole schools of thought and interpretation have grown up around George's actions and the motives behind them. Whigs vs. Tories, court supporters vs. court opponents, George's desire to return to the divine right of kings vs. parliament's attempts to usurp power from the throne.

But whichever side of these arguments seems more persuasive, they were matters of domestic politics.

Over the 75 years between the founding of Jamestown in 1607 under James I and the chartering of Pennsylvania 75 years later under Charles II, even the granting of charters often hinged on domestic or economic considerations. New England was a good place to ship religious dissents. New Jersey was a nice gift to the king's brother. Pennsylvania paid off an old royal debt. Georgia, funded in 1732, was almost purely a domestic consideration—a place for those people economically ruined by the South Sea Bubble and a buffer against the Spanish to the south.

During the decade of political unrest that followed George III's accession in 1760 until Lord North became prime minister in 1770, England was, in Brooke's words, "Like a sailing ship faced with a heavy wind, the British government tacked one way and then another but always headed in the same direction."²

From Bute to Grenville to Rockingham to Pitt to Grafton, prime ministers were replaced on the basis of domestic questions that were tangential to the North American colonies at best.

Even if we accept Miller's explanation that "the divine right of kings had been succeeded by the divine right of parliament and parliament was displaying 'a kingly fondness for prerogative.' It was the refusal of the Americans to bow before this new divinity that precipitated the American Revolution."³ it is still basically a matter of a domestic struggle between king and parliament with the colonies caught in the crossfire.

"If there is one event in history which can truly be described as inevitable," Brooke writes⁴, "it is the political separation between Great Britain and her American colonies. What was not inevitable was the way in which the separation came about."

The way the separation came about, it seems to the author, was the inability of either side to find any sort of middle ground between Britain's vision of herself as ruler of the world and the Americans' vision of their future.

As Ferling summarizes it, "Too many issues were decided in London, where the interests of the residents of the mother country outweighed those of the provincials."⁵

Endnotes

CHAPTER 1

1. Palmer & Colton, p. 249
2. Palmer & Colton, p. 273
3. MacManus, p. 491
4. A History of the Irish Race
5. Harlow, p. 58
6. MacManus, p. 492
7. Current, Williams p. 52
8. Current, Williams p. 88
9. Knollenberg, p. 138
10. Knollenberg p. 142
11. Bruckenberger p. 12
12. Craik, as quoted by Harlow pp. 23-24

CHAPTER 2

1. Encyclopedia Brittanica
2. Strong, p. 186

3. Murray, p. 98
4. As quoted by Strong, p. 190

CHAPTER 3

1. Howard, pp. 10-11
2. Strong, p. 306
3. Hofstadtler, p. 16
4. Hofstadtler, p. 17

CHAPTER 4

1. Original text
2. Boorstin, p. 7
3. Boorstin, p. 8
4. An Outline of American History
5. An Outline of American History, Chapter 2
6. Hofstadtler, p. 151
7. Hofstadtler, p. 135
8. As quoted, Hofstadtler, p. 136
9. Hofstadtler, p. 149
10. Hofstadtler, p. 141
11. Taylor, p. 130
12. ibid
13. Taylor, p. 134
14. Allen, p. 146
15. Hofstadtler, pp. 8-9
16. Hofstadtler, p. 67
17. Webnotes, Chapter 5
18. North American Colonies, Section 6
19. Allen, p. 143
20. Hofstadtler, p. 71
21. Allen, p. 142
22. ibid

23 Hofstadtler. P. 72
24 Shama, p. 402
25 Shama, p. 416
26 Hofstadtler, p. 73
27 Weeden, W.B., Economic and Social History of New England, 1890, II, p. 459
28 Hofstadtler, p. 72
29 op cit, p. 73
30 Webnotes, Chapter 4
31 Hostadtler, p. 66
32 Hofstadtler, p. 6
33 MacManus, p. 483
34 Palfrey, Vol. II, p. 393
35 Reid, pp. 28-29
36 Howard, p. 17
37 Beer, p. 154
38 Reid, pp. 28-29
39 ibid
40 Bancroft, quoted by Harlow, p. 16
41 Howard, p. 18
42 Hibbert, p. 117

CHAPTER 5

1 Close & Burke, p. 227
2 Beard, p.91
3 Americana, Vol. V, p. 456
4 Adams, p. 244
5 Fuller, Vol. II, p. 217
6 Starr et al, p. 227
7 Fuller, p. 220
8 ibid, p. 224
9 Bl;um, et al, p. 82
10 Ridpath, Vol. II, pp. 298-99
11 Watson, Vol. I, p. 650

[12] Todd & Curti, p. 48
[13] Ridpath, Vol. II, p. 307
[14] Beard, p. 91
[15] Franklin, as quoted J.C. Miller, p. 43
[16] Beard, p. 92
[17] Ferling, p. 14
[18] As quoted, Morison & Commager, p. 8
[19] Blum et al, p. 81
[20] Ogg, p. 140
[21] Henderson, Vol. II, p. 148
[22] ibid, pp. 149-50
[23] Churchill, Vol. III, p. 104
[24] Ogg, p. 141
[25] Ogg, p. 140
[26] Henderson, Vol. II, p. 151

CHAPTER 6

[1] Watson, Vol. I, p.650
[2] Fuller, Vol. II, p. 250
[3] Parkman, Vol. I, p. 187
[4] Encyclopedia Americana
[5] Watson, Vol. I, p. 650
[6] ibid, p. 650
[7] Parkman, Vol. I, p. 184
[8] Churchill, Vol. III, p. 114
[9] Strong, p. 327
[10] Mahan, p. 285
[11] Churchill, Vol. III, p. 114
[12] Mahan, p. 286
[13] Ibid, p. 286-88
[14] Watson, Vol. I, p. 650
[15] Churchill, Vol. III, p. 114
[16] ibid

17 Lapevrouse-Bonbfils, Histoire de la Marine, as quoted by Mahan, p. 288
18 Churchill, Vol. III, p. 114
19 Encyclopedia Brittanica, Vol. V, p. 319
20 Higginbotham, p. 20
21 Churchill, Vol. III, p. 125
22 Strong, p. 330
23 Andrews, p. 450
24 Churchill, Vol. III, p. 1124
25 ibid
26 ibid
27 Fuller, Vol. II, p. 245
28 Andrews, p. 451
29 Encyclopedia Americana, Vol. XX, p. 395
30 Parkman, Vol. I, p. 412
31 Churchill, Vol. II, p. 126
32 Parkman, Vol. II, p. 51
33 Blum et al, p. 84
34 Encyclopedia Americana, Vol. V, p. 456
35 Parkman, Vol. II, p. 134
36 Ridpath, Vol. II, p. 333
37 ibid, p. 334
38 ibid, p. 339
39 ibid
40 Watson, p. 652

CHAPTER 7

1 SWhite, p. 54
2 Ayling, p. 17
3 ibid, p. 22
4 Brooke, p. 17
5 Ayling, p. 19
6 Encyclopedia Britannica, Vol. X, p. 185

7. Brooke, p. 22
8. ibid, p. 18
9. ibid, p. 22
10. Ayling, p. 31
11. Blum et al, p. 85
12. Ayling, p. 20
13. Encyclopedia Brtitannica, Vol. X, p. 185
14. Brooke, p. 30
15. Ayling, p.35
16. As quoted by Brooke, p. 18
17. Ayling, p. 32
18. Brooke, p. 26
19. Srong, p. 359
20. Brooke, p.45
21. Churchill, Vol. III, p. 276-77

CHAPTER 8

1. Ayling, p. 43
2. Churchill, p. 30
3. Clarke, pp. 276-77
4. Strong, p. 330
5. Churchill, Vol. III, p. 98
6. White, p. 37
7. Churchill, Vol. III, p. 130
8. White, p. 42
9. Butterfield, p. 64
10. Hibbert, p. 35
11. Churchill, Vol. III, p. 131
12. Durants, p. 689
13. Ayling, p. 89
14. White, p. 19
15. Churchill, Vol. III, p. 130
16. Ayling, p. 88
17. White, p. 18

18 White, p. 30
19 Ayling, p. 89
20 Ayling, p. 97
21 Churchill, Vol. III, pp.132-33
22 Brooke, p. 93
23 Brooke, p. 94
24 Brooke, p. 95
25 Brooke, p. 101
26 Pares, p. 81
27 Brooke, p. 101

CHAPTER 9

1 William Miller, p. 97
2 Degler, p. 76
3 Churchill, Vol. III, p. 133
4 Ayling, p. 88
5 Churchill, Vol. III, p. 133
6 ibid, p. 134
7 Bartlett, p. 6
8 ibid
9 Corbett, Vol. II, p.173
10 Channing, Vol. II, p. 603
11 Howard, p. 7
12 Encyclopedia Americana
13 Bartlett, p. 7
14 ibid, p. 4
15 ibid, pp. 7-10
16 J.C. Miller, p. 191
17 Bartlett, p. 11
18 Churchill, Vol. III, p. 133
19 White, p. 64
20 ibid, p. 64
21 As quoted by White, p. 64
22 J.C. Miller, p. 82

CHAPTER 10

1. Henderson, Vol. II, p. 181
2. Morrison & Commager, p. 2
3. Mahan, p. 291
4. Henderson, Vol. II, p. 181
5. Ayling, p. 97
6. Ayling, pp. 101-102
7. Ayling, p. 93
8. Brooke, p. 79
9. A Web of English History
10. Ayling, p. 101
11. Prof. David A. Sklansky, UCLA School of Law
12. Howard,. p. 102
13. Ayling, p. 107
14. Ayling, p. 110
15. Reid, p. 28
16. Reid, p. 12
17. Reid, p. 12
18. Reid, p. 13
19. As quoted, Knollenberg, p. 51
20. Reid, p. 14
21. Reid, p. 19
22. McCullough, p. 61
23. Howard, p. 103
24. Knollenberg, p. 128
25. As quoted, Howard, p. 111
25. Biographical Dictionary of Pennsylvania Legislators
27. Encyclopedia of American History, p. 73

CHAPTER 11

1. Bowen, p. 253
2. White. P. 93

3   or £300,000. Howard, p. 104
4   or £100,000, Howard, p. 104
5   Brian Tubbs, *Money & Mayhem*
6   White, p. 95
7   White, p. 86
8   As quoted, White, p. 86
9   Knox, *The Claim of the Colonies*, as quoted, Howard, p. 125
10 Bowen, p. 254
11 As quoted, Bowen, p. 262
12 Howard, p. 136
13 As quoted in Howard, p. 127
14 As quoted in Howard, pp. 130-131
15 Howard, p. 132
16 Howard p. 136
17 White, p. 89
18 J.C. Miller, p. 25
19 White, p. 85
20 Howard, p. 142
21 Howard, p. 144
22 Knollenberg, p. 65
23 As quoted, Howard, p. 150
24 Howard, p. 153
25 Miller, p. 132
26 ibid
27 As quoted, Miller, p. 135
28 Brooke, p. 119
29 Or 27, per Howard, p. 154
30 As quoted, Howard, p. 155

CHAPTER 12

1   Miller, p. 143
2   Miller, p. 140
3   Ayling, p. 134
4   Ayling, p. 135

5   Lecky, England II, p. 362, as quoted in Howard, p. 163
6   As quoted, Howard, p. 167
7   Brooke, p. 129
8   ibid
9   Ayling, p. 137
10 Miller, p. 158
11 Miller, pp, 162-3
12 Miller, p. 164
13 As quoted, Knollenberg, p. 163
14 White, p. 115
15 White, p. 117
16 Brooke, p. 124
17 White, p. 118
18 As quoted, White, p. 119
19 Brooke, p. 135
20 ibid
21 Brooke, p. 139
22 ibid
23 Miller, p. 151
24 Ayling, p. 146
25 White, p. 123
26 ibid

CHAPTER 13

1   Miller, p. 211
2   White. p. 128
3   Miller, p. 261
4   Miller, p. 171
5   As quoted, Miller, pp. 171-2
6   Miller, p. 202
7   As quoted, Miller, p. 187
8   Miller, p. 262
9   Howard, p. 193
10 Letters, Vol. III, London, 1757-1775

[11] White, p. 132
[12] Brooke, p. 154
[13] ibid
[14] White, p. 150

CHAPTER 14

[1] As quoted, White, p. 152
[2] Brooke, p. 161
[3] Hibbert, p. 139
[4] Howard, p. 244
[5] Zobel, p. 178
[6] ibid, p. 180
[7] Howard, p. 205
[8] Churchill, p. 176
[9] As quoted, Zobel, p. 214
[10] Howard, p. 244
[11] Taylor, p. 311
[12] North, as quoted, Knollenberg, p. 244
[13] Howard, p. 244
[14] Shama, p. 409
[15] Howard, p. 245
[16] Howard, p. 248
[17] Rhode Island Committee for the Humanities
[18] Morison & Commager, p. 50
[19] Brooke, p. 174
[20] Churchill, Vol. III, p. 179
[21] Brooke, p. 174
[22] As quoted, Brooke, p. 176

CHAPTER 15

[1] Ayling, p. 243
[2] ibid, p. 243

3   ibid
4   As quoted, Howard, p. 261
5   Howard, p. 265
6   Miller, p. 380
7   Miller, pp. 380-81
8   Brooke, p. 175
9   Ayling, p. 247
10 Miller, p. 388
11 Hildreth, as quoted, Howard, p. 297
12 Brooke, p. 175
13 As quoted, Howard, p. 305
14 Ketchum, p. 18
15 Commager & Morris, p. 71
16 Commager & Morris, p. 74

CHAPTER 16

1   Commager & Morris, p. 70
2   Howard, p. 311
3   Commager & Morris, pp. 96-97
4   As quoted, Ketchum, p. 45
5   As quoted, Seymour, p. 44
6   Gruber, p. 59
7   Commager & Morris, p. 231
8   Ayling, p. 247
9   Seymour, p. 33
10 As quoted, Ayling, p. 248
11 Seymour, p. 34
12 Seymour, p. 33
13 Seymour, p. 58
14 ibid
15 Seymour, p. 59
16 Ayling, p. 250
17 Ketchum, p. 6
18 Ferling, p. 183

[19] Commager & Morris, p. 178
[20] Ferling, pp. 183-4
[21] Commager & Morris, p. 182
[22] ibid, p. 180
[23] ibid, p. 183
[24] Ferling, p. 184
[25] Ayling, p. 252
[26] Ridpath, Vol. III, p. 384
[27] Commager & Morris, p. 427
[28] ibid
[29] Ridpath, Vol. III, p. 384
[30] McCullough, p. 157
[31] ibid
[32] ibid, p. 158
[33] McCullough, p. 158

EPILOGUE

[1] Schlesinger, p. 170
[2] Brooke, p. 171
[3] Miller, pp. 216-17
[4] Brooke, p. 170
[5] Ferling, p. 82

Bibliography

Adams, George Burton: The Growth of the French Nation, N.Y., 1924.
Andrews, Charles M.: A History of England, Boston, 1983.
Angle, Paul M. (Ed), By These Words, N.Y. 1954.
Ayling, Stanley: George III, N.Y., 1972.
Bailey, Thomas: Annals of Nottinghamshire, London, 1853.
Bartlett, Ruhl J. (Ed): The Record of American Diplomacy, N.Y., 1947.
Barnard, T.C.:Cromwellian Ireland, N.Y., 2000
Barzun, Jacques: The Modern Researcher, N.Y., 1957.
Beard, Charles A.: A New Basic History of the United States, N.Y., 1960.
Beatty, John Louis & Johnson: Heritage of Western Civilization,
Bedford, Henry F., & Colbourn: The Americans, N.Y., 1972.
Benton, William (Ed:): The Annals of America, Chicago, 1968.
Bishop, Jim: The Birth of the United States, N.Y., 1976.
Bliven, Bruce Jr., Under the Guns, N.Y., 1972
Blum, John M.: The National Experience, 2nd Edition, N.Y., 1968.

Blum, John M.: The Promise of America, Boston, 1966.
Boorstin, Daniel J.: The Americans; The Colonial Experience, N.Y., 1966.
Bowen, Catherine Drinker: John Adams and the American Revolution, Old Saybrook, Conn., 1979
Brooke, John: King George III, N.Y., 1972.
Brown, Robert E.; Charles Beard and the Constitution, Princeton, 1956.
Brown, Stuart Gerry: Alexander Hamilton, N.Y., 1967.
Bruckenberger, R.L.: Image of America, N.Y., 1959,
Butterfield, Herbert: George III and the Historians, N.Y., 1969.
Channing, : History of the United States, 1920.
Cheney, E.P.: A Short History of England, Boston, 1904.
Churchill, Winston: A History of the English Speaking People, N.Y., 1963.
Close, Upton: The Ladder of History, N.Y., 1945.
Commager, Henry Steele (Ed.): The Spirit of Seventy-Six, N.Y., 1975.
Conygham, David Power: Ireland Past and Present, N.Y., 1885.
Colbourn, Trevor, & Bedford: The Americans, N.Y., 1972.
Cooke Alistair: America, N.Y., 1973.
Cronin, Vincent: Louis & Antoinette, N.Y., 1974.
Cunliffe, Marcus: George Washington, Man and Monument, N.Y., 1958
Current, Richard N. (with Williams & Freidel): American History: A Survey, N.Y., 1975
Dangerfield, George: The Damnable Question, N.Y., 1976.
Davis, Burke: A Williamsburg Galaxy, N.Y., 1968.
Degler, Carl N.: Out of Our Past, N.Y., 1959.
DePew, Chauncey (Ed.): The Library of Oratory, N.Y., 1902.
Dietz, Frederick C.: Political and Social History of England, New York, 1948
Durant, Will & Ariel: Rousseau and the Revolution, N.Y., 1967.

Eckert, Allan W.: Wilderness Empire, N.Y., 1971.
Eliot, Charles M. (Ed.): American Historical Documents, N.Y., 1938.
Eyre, Louisa Lear (Ed.): Letters and Recollections of George Washington, N.Y., 1932.
Faulkner, Antonia (Ed): The Lives of the Kings and Queens of England, N.Y., 1975.
Faulkner, Harold U.: American Political and Social History, N.Y., 1948
Ferber, Mark F.: Government and Politics in the United States, N.Y., 1965.
Ferling, John: A Leap in the Dark, New York, 2003
Franklin, Benjamin: The Autobiography of, N.Y., 1965.
Fuller, Maj. Gen. J.F.C.: A Military History of the Western World, N.Y., 1955.
Galvin, John R.: Three Men of Boston, Washington, 1976.
Halleck, Rueben: Our Nation's Heritage, N.Y., 1931.
Harlow, Ralph Volney: The Growth of the United States, N.Y., 1943.
Hart, Albert Bushnell: Commonwealth History of Massachusetts, N.Y., 1927.
Hathorn, Guy B.: Government and Politics in the United States, N.J., 1965.
Henderson, Ernest F.: A Short History of Germany, N.Y., 1920.
Hibbert, Christopher: George III, New York, 1998
Higginbotham, Don: The War of American Independence, N.Y., 1971.
Hofstadter, Richard: America at 1750, N.Y., 1971.
Howard, George Elliott: Preliminaries of the Revolution, N.Y., 1970 Ed.
Isaacson, Walter: Benjamin Franklin, N.Y., 2003
Josephy, Alvin M. (Ed.): The American Heritage Book of Indians, N.Y., 1961.
Ketchum, Richard M.: Decisive Day, N.Y., 1974.
Knollenberg, Bernhard: Origin of the American Revolution, N.Y., 1960.

Labaree, Bejamin W.: America's Nation-Time, Boston, 1972.
Lancaster, Bruce: The American Heritage Book of the Revolution, N.Y., 1971.
Leyburn, James G.: The Scotch Irish, Chapel Hill, 1962.
Mabie, Dr. Hamilton: Giants of the Republic, N.Y., 1895.
Magnusson, Magnus: Scotland: The Story of a Nation, N.Y., 2000
Mahan, Alfred Thayer: The Influence of Sea Power on History, 12th edition, Boston.
Marshall, Thomas M.: American History, N.Y., 1936.
Matloff, Maurice (Ed.): American Military History, Washington, D.C., 1968.
May, Henry: A Synopsis of American History, Chicago, 1976.
McCullough, David: John Adams, New York, 2001
McFarland, Philip: The Brave Bostonians, Boulder, Colo, 1998.
McManus, Seumas: The Story of the Irish Race, N.Y., 1969.
Middlekauff, Robert: The Glorious Cause, New York, 1982
Miller, John C.: Origins of the American Revolution, N.Y., 1943.
Miller, John C.: The First Frontier, N.Y., 1971.
Miller, William: A New History of the United States, N.Y. 1971.
Mitchell, William A.: Outlines of the World's Military History, Penn., 1940.
Morison, Samuel Eliot: The Growth of the American Republic, N.Y., 1930.
Morris, Charles R. (Ed.): Burke's Speech on Conciliation, N.Y., 1945.
Morris, Richard B. (Ed.): Encyclopedia of American History, N.Y., 1953.
Morris, Richard B. & Commager: The Spirit of Seventy-Six, N.Y., 1975.
Mott, Frank Luther; American Journalism, N.Y., 1947.
Nef, John U.: War and Human Progress, Boston, 1950.
O'Connor, Thomas H.: The Boston Irish, Boston, 1995.
Ogg. David: Europe of the Ancien Regime, N.Y., 1965.

Paine, Thomas: Common Sense and the Crisis, N.Y., 1960.
Parkman, Francis: Montcalm and Wolfe, Boston, 1925.
Parkman, Francis: Pioneers of France in the New World, Boston, 1907
Pearson, Michael: Those Damned Rebels, 1972.
Penniman, Howard R.: Government and Politics in the United States, N.J., 1965.
Plum, J.H.: The American Heritage Book of the Revolution, N.Y.,1971.
Rankin, Hugh F.: Rebels and Redcoats, N.Y., 1975.
Reid, John Phillip: The Authority to Tax, Wisconsin, 1987
Rhodehamel, John (ed): The American Revolution., New York, 2001
Ridpath, John C.: History of the United States, N.Y., 1902.
Rifkin, Shepard: The Savage Years, Conn., 1967.
Roberts, Kenneth: March to Quebec, N.Y., 1946.
Rowen, Herbert F. (Ed.): From Absolutism to Revolution, 1648-1848, N.Y., 1963.
Schama, Simon: A History of Britain, Vol, II, N.Y., 2001
Scheer, George F.: Rebels and Redcoats, N.Y., 1975.
Schlesinger, Arthur Meier: New Viewpoints on American History, N.Y., 1922.
Sellars, Charles M.: A Synopsis of American History, Chicago, 1976.
Seymour, William: The Price of Folly, London, 1995.
Smith, Adam: Wealth of Nations, N.Y., 1937.
Smith, Page: A People's History of the American Revolution, N.Y. 1976.
Starr, Charles G.: Rebels and Redcoats, N.Y., 1975.
Stokesbury, James L.: A Short History of the American Revolution, N.Y., 1991.
Taylor, Alan: American Colonies, New York, 2001
Thatcher, B.B.: Indian Biography, Akron, 1910.
Todd, Lewis P.: Rise of the America Nation, N.Y., 1964.
Trevelyan, Sir George Otto: The American Revolution, N.Y., 1964.

Trevelyan, G.M.: History of England, N.Y., 1953.
VanDoran, Carl: The Secret History of the American Revolution, N.Y., 1941.
Vuillemier, Marion: Indians on Olde Cape Cod, Taunton, 1970.
Watson, Thomas E.: The Story of France, London, 1904.
Webb, Stephen Saunders: Lord Churchill's Coup, N.Y., 1995.
Wells, H.G.: The Outline of History, N.Y., 1949.
White, R.J.: The Age of George III, N.Y., 1969.
Wood, Gordon S.: The Creation of the American Republic, Chapel Hill, 1969.
Zink, Harold: Modern Governments, Princeton, 1965.
Zobel, Hiller B.: The Boston Massacre, N.Y., 1970.

ENCYCLOPEDIAS AND PERIODICALS:

Americana, 1958 edition.
Britannica, 1951 edition.
Rand McNally Atlas of World History, N.Y., 1957.
British History Illustrated, 6-7/76, pp. 6-13.
Treasury of the World's Great Speeches, N.Y., 1965.
Encyclopedia of American Facts and Dates, N.Y., 1966.